The MUSTARDSEEDS

E . M . WILKIE

THE MUSTARDSEEDS

Aletheia Adventure Series Book 4

Book 1 of the Battle for Aletheia Trilogy

E M Wilkie

JOHN RITCHIE LTD
CHRISTIAN PUBLICATIONS

Copyright © 2015 by John Ritchie Ltd.
40 Beansburn, Kilmarnock, Scotland

www.ritchiechristianmedia.co.uk

ISBN-13: 978 1 910513 18 7

Written by E M Wilkie
Illustrated by E M Wilkie
www.aletheiabooks.co
Copyright © 2015

Cover illustration by Graeme Hewitson.
Interior illustrations are by E M Wilkie.

To Zach, Bobby, Seth, and Harry,

This story was written in the hope that you will have

faith in God, even faith the size of a mustard seed.

"If you have faith as a mustard seed…

nothing will be impossible for you."

Matthew 17:20

PREFACE

This story is an attempt to help and encourage young readers to develop an understanding of the truth contained in the Word of God, the Bible. However, all characters, places, descriptions and incidents are entirely fictional and this adventure story is not intended to be a substitute for the teaching contained in the Bible, but rather an aid to understanding. The illustrations and allegories used in this story are not perfect; and therefore, whilst it is hoped that readers will benefit from the truth and lessons developed in this story, they must be urged to develop an understanding of Bible truth and doctrine from the Bible alone.

The author would like to acknowledge the invaluable help and advice of the following people who assisted in the production of this book:

M J Wilkie, E Taylor, R Hatt, A Henderson, R Chesney, and Margareta.

Many thanks to you all.

Contents

9

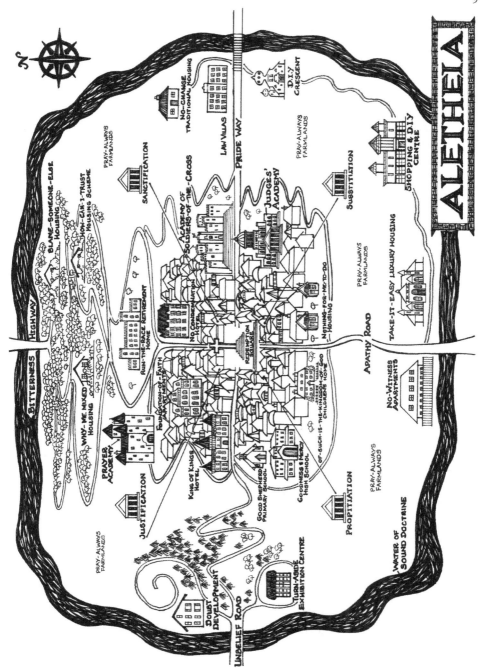

ALETHEIA

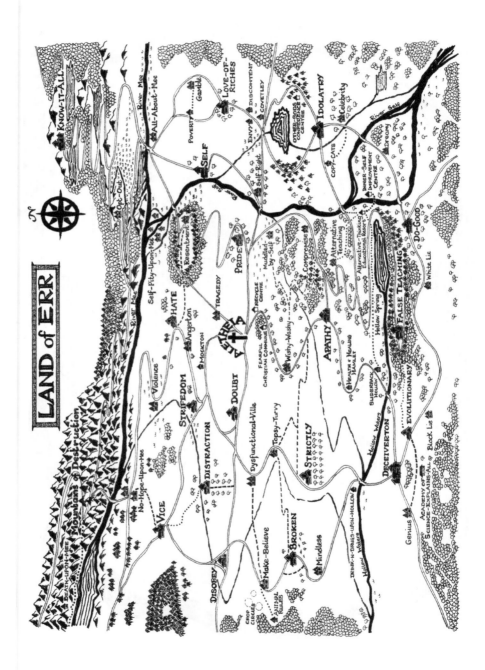

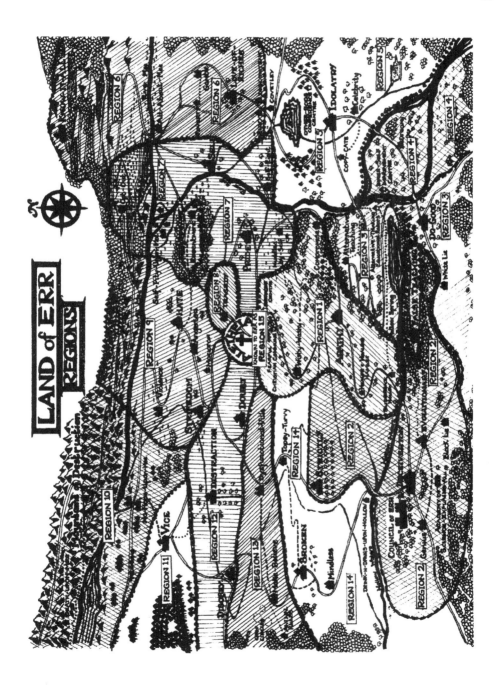

PROLOGUE

At last they were assembled. It was no easy task to gather fourteen members of the Council of Err for a formal Government Meeting. Many of the Regions of the land of Err were so hopelessly disorganised, chaotic, or downright rebellious that it usually took bribery or threats of something particularly nasty to get them together.

But this time they had a shared goal.

Governor Genie, who was the elected Governor in charge of the Council of Err, and who therefore ruled the land of Err, was the representative of Region 2, where the Government was based. Region 2 included the cities of Deceiverton, Genius, and Evolutionary, where the most intelligent people lived. No one could trust the word of anyone from Region 2, but they proved to be the most efficient, organised, and cunning Region in the entire land. The other Regions weren't sure how it happened, but somehow these clever, deceiving towns always sat in the seat of Government.

Governor Genie was the most normal-looking person at the gathering of the Council of Err. She was immaculate, tailored, clean and tidy. She had the smile of a diplomat and the smooth-tongue of a peacemaker. She was the only person there who could extract something meaningful from the meeting, even if she made it up afterwards. She completely despised the vast majority of other Council members.

Governor Genie got to her feet and smiled a bright smile of welcome, hiding the revulsion she felt for the representative from Region 13, who had unfortunately moved his seat to the space directly at her right hand. The Region 13 representative came from the town of Make-Believe; he looked like he had come dressed for a fancy-dress party – although whether he intended to represent an animal or a person was not clear. He smelt like something from a farmyard.

The chairs at the table were curiously in tune with the representatives who claimed them, and the chair that Make-Believe claimed didn't fit neatly at the table at all. It was like something from another planet – a spaceship with flashing lights and additional arms and legs sticking out at inconvenient angles. Governor Genie had to avoid the flashing arm of the chair which moved continually, waving around as if it had something to say. It was just about the worst chair to be next to, but seating was always a hazard at Council of Err meetings.

Governor Genie noticed that the northern Regions, 9, 10, and 11, had unfortunately contrived to sit together again. They preferred fighting to talking; whether it was with each other, or with the softer southern Regions, they did not care.

The representative of Region 8, from the town of Tragedy, was tear-stained and being consoled by the Region 7 representative, who this year was a woman from the town of Resentment. She sat on a chair with sharp spikes sticking in odd, unexpected directions, pricking anyone who came too close. Governor Genie wondered if she could ensure 7 and 8 didn't sit together at future meetings. They were very bad for each other.

The representative of Region 9, a man from Mockton, had already elaborately removed a large handkerchief and was blowing his nose and pretending to cry, whilst eyeing weeping Tragedy with a cruel smile.

Region 1, represented by a most unhelpful woman from Compromise, who generally agreed with everything that was said, sniggered at the man from Mockton, who thoroughly enjoyed the attention. Compromise's chair had four completely different legs and was distinctly off the straight – which meant she sat on a slope and was constantly trying to stay on her seat.

Region 4 was represented by a woman from Dreamy – who was seated in an armchair which contained dozens of plump, downy cushions. She perpetually gave the impression of being in a trance, but, fortunately, she was not sat next to the Region 14 representative who was from the town of Drink-n-Drugs-Upon-Hollow. *She* had bright pink hair and glazed eyes; she was already nearly asleep on her beanbag seat which was almost beneath the table. If she and Dreamy were sat together, all they did was whisper about visions and dreams.

The remaining representatives were passable, although the representative from Know-It-All always talked far too much and had an opinion on just about everything that was said. He sat on a chair several inches higher than anyone else, clearly considering himself superior to those around.

But there was one notable absence at the meeting. The last seat at the long, wide table, a sturdy, stable chair with a back shaped like a book, was the chair for the representative from Region 15. There was a surprisingly prosperous, peaceful, fruitful city in the centre of the land, known to its people as *Aletheia*. To the people of Err it was a city full of unknown riches and mysteries. They called it Region 15. But the seat at the table belonging to Region 15 had never been filled.

And now it had become imperative that it was.

Governor Genie guided the meeting with careful delicacy. She was used to the idiosyncrasies of the Regions of Err. And, on the matter they had gathered to discuss, the matter of the 'Revolting Nations Agreement', they were unusually united. "We must work together on this matter," she said earnestly. "The proposed Agreement with other revolting nations – our neighbours and friends, some of whom share our borders – is a wonderful opportunity to forge lasting ties, particularly with the important land of Iniquitous. Trade, finance, technology; new food and materials and substances; science, inventions, religions – all of these could be developed in ways we can't possibly imagine, *if* we sign up to the Agreement!"

"I think we're already convinced of that," said the man from Mockton sarcastically. "We all know about the riches and benefits that will come from entering the Agreement with Iniquitous. It's Region 15 you need to persuade!"

The representative from Region 10, a terrible, awesome-looking man from the Mountains of Destruction, growled angrily at the reference to the stubbornness of Region 15. "Just smash them to smithereens!" he muttered.

"I once had a vision about the land of Iniquitous," said Dreamy, in her slow, mesmerising voice.

"*Dreams* are all very well for people who just sit around and *do nothing* all day!" snapped Resentment.

"I appreciate that *we're* all cooperating with the plan to sign up to the Agreement," said the Governor hastily, trying not to get sidetracked into yet another pointless quarrel. "And we do appreciate *you* all being willing to be the regional representatives who will make up our Team WondERRful and sign the Agreement. But we *must* have a representative from Region 15! Otherwise we cannot be part of the Agreement with Iniquitous and other nations."

"Why don't we just pulverise the whole of Region 15?!" muttered the man from the Mountains of Destruction. "Then it won't matter!"

"Are you *quite certain* we can't sign the Revolting Nations Agreement without a representative from Region 15?" asked Know-It-All.

"Surprising you don't know the answer yourself," sniggered Mockton.

The girl from Drink-n-Drugs snored softly from somewhere beneath the table.

The Governor read from a piece of paper which contained the rules of signing the Agreement. *"Every region in a land must pledge itself to the Revolting Nations Agreement, and have an agreed representative to sign on their behalf. Only then can a nation sign up to, and benefit from, the Agreement."*

"Can I see those rules?" asked Know-It-All. "I might be able to shed further light on what they mean."

Governor Genie ignored his request.

"I don't see why people from *Know-It-All* always think *they* know better than the rest of us!" objected Resentment.

"Perhaps there's a clue in the name," muttered Mockton.

"Why can't we just make up our own rules for signing the Agreement?" suggested Make-Believe.

"I'm sure there are a number of options we could explore!" said Compromise brightly.

"Perhaps the answer will come to me in a vision," murmured Dreamy.

"I don't think we *can* sign this Agreement according to the rules the Governor read," said the representative of Region 12 tremulously. He was a mild-mannered man from the town of Doubt – who always did precisely that.

"Enough!" growled the man from Region 11, Vice. "We all agreed we want to benefit from Iniquitous. We'll sign this Agreement, even if we have to cheat and *make* it happen!"

"How can you *make* the Agreement happen?" asked Doubt. "If the city of Aletheia – so-called Region 15..."

"Stop saying the name of that city!" growled Destruction. "I hate their name! They're a Region – the same as the rest of us!"

"It's been called Region 15 for hundreds of years!" interposed the representative from Region 3, a woman from White Lie who was always imprecise about the truth.

"I don't see why Region 15 should keep its name – Aletheia – when we all had to give ours up for Region numbers!" snapped Resentment.

"The people from Aletheia are very kind to us," murmured Tragedy.

"Very kind indeed. I wouldn't want anything bad to happen to..."

"Oooh! Boo-hoo-hoo!" said Mockton rudely, sniggering when Tragedy howled with frustration.

"We'll do anything it takes to sign that Agreement!" growled Vice. "Go to war against Region 15! Invade them! Overcome them!"

"Grind them to dust!" interrupted Destruction with relish.

"We *will have* a representative from Region 15 for Team WondERRful! We *will sign* that Agreement!" concluded Vice.

"I really don't see how," mumbled Doubt meekly.

The Governor thought it was time to intervene. "You all make valid points," she said smoothly, which wasn't remotely true. "I appreciate all your suggestions..." which was equally untrue, "...and we will consider them all in due course..." which was a bare-faced lie. "We must all act together to persuade our esteemed colleagues from the, uh, so far uncooperative Region 15, of the value of signing the Agreement," finished the Governor. She was still smiling, but she thought, as she always did, that discussions in the Council of Err were utterly pointless, and that dictatorship by Region 2 was so much more efficient. She had all the answers – she just needed the regional representatives' cooperation with the Revolting Nations Agreement, and, if necessary, their help in dealing with Region 15 too.

Of course, she wouldn't explain the details to the other Regions. Most of them barely believed in the tiny creatures of Err that, unbeknown to them, had already set things in motion against the great, coveted city of Aletheia.

The plan of the Meddlers was controlled from laboratories in Region 2; known and approved by the Governor of Err. The land of Err had, at last, discovered the secret of the strength of Aletheia. They would target prayer! The Meddlers and their cohorts – the Fretters – would soon bring Region 15 to its knees.

No longer would Aletheia be allowed to defy the wishes of the land of Err, which it had so long withstood. No longer would Aletheia provoke the Council of Err with its stubborn message about the Truth of the Bible. It must *not* be allowed to stand in the way of the signing of the all-important Revolting Nations Agreement. Err *would* have a pact with the terrible but exciting and important land of Iniquitous in the north.

And one day, soon, Aletheia would be overcome.

CHAPTER 1

THE PLAN OF THE MEDDLERS

Hezekiah Wallop knew eavesdropping was wrong. Children weren't meant to listen at closed doors to adults' secret conversations. But this was no ordinary time; and this was no ordinary conversation. Strange things were happening in his home city of Aletheia. They were small things, but Hezekiah knew the small things mounted up to something sinister and worrying and just plain *bad*. It was because of these things, this vague threat to the city, that important managers went to private Management Meetings and held secret conversations behind closed doors. It was because of this that his father, Mr Hardy Wallop, Superintendent of Entry to Aletheia, was talking on the Mission Link in his private study in the family's top floor home at Foundation-of-Faith Apartments. Of course, Hezekiah couldn't hear the whole conversation, just one side of it, and even that was a bit disjointed. He heard something about an "increase in the numbers of Fretters", mention of "decrease in prayer cover from Run-the-Race Retirement Home", the term "significant effect on The Outskirts", and again and again the expression "the plan of the Meddlers". But that was nothing new. Nearly everybody in Aletheia knew the worry in the city was because of the 'plan of the Meddlers[1]'.

Some people shrugged it off. What could tiny, pesky, flying imps called Meddlers do against the might of the city which stood for the truth of the Word of God, the Bible[2]? Other people shut themselves away and pretended it wasn't happening. But the group of Managers, and Heads, and Chiefs, and Directors of all the important departments in the whole of Aletheia, planned for the defence of the city as if the threat was very serious and certainly too great to ignore.

Of course, there wasn't much the Christian kids in the city could do. That was the worst of it. They just picked up incidental snippets of information from the adults; they didn't know how they could defend the city of Aletheia against the nefarious plan of the Meddlers. That's why Hezekiah, and his twin brother and sister, Hugo and Henrietta, and his cousin, Josie Faithful, and a few other Christian friends who didn't laugh at the puny Meddlers, were looking forward to school this morning. Mr Philologus Mustardpot, the formidable Head of Education, was going to address the whole school. There was speculation that the kids would, at last, know all about the plan of the Meddlers for the downfall of the city of Truth.

Hezekiah quietly left Foundation-of-Faith Apartments before anyone else – apart from his busy father – was even awake. Hezekiah was going to visit his friend, Mr Croft Straw, at his Pray-Always farm. Hezekiah was very keen on farming and he was allowed to go to Mr Straw's farm to help with the chores before school began.

It was a glorious spring day when he set off across the city. Winter, which had been particularly severe, was very late in giving way to spring. In fact, spring was so delayed that the farmers of the Pray-Always Farmlands were worried that they would be late planting their crops, and *that* might mean a food shortage for the city. It was very important for the Christians who lived in Aletheia to eat the right food: only food grown on the Pray-Always Farmlands was suitable for Christians to eat. But now the long winter was past. All around Aletheia, and across the fields that spread out around the city, right to the boundary formed by the Water of Sound Doctrine, the sun was shining, and new green shoots and buds and leaves were opening in abundance.

The city was mostly at rest when Hezekiah – accompanied by his faithful dog, Hector – entered the narrow streets. Only Mrs De Voté was awake, and she was opening her Faithful shop in the early morning sunshine. She was often there when Hezekiah set off for the farm.

"Good morning, Zek," she said. She was now on nickname terms with Hezekiah.

"Good morning, Mrs De Voté," he returned politely.

"And good morning to Hector too, of course," she added, glancing at the dog rather more warily. Young though he was, Hector was already becoming somewhat notorious amongst the people in this part of Aletheia.

Zek didn't notice that Mrs De Voté was less than pleased to see his beloved dog; he was just delighted whenever Hector was acknowledged. "He caught a mouse on Mr Straw's farm yesterday," he said proudly.

"Did he?" said Mrs De Voté. "Perhaps you could teach him to catch Meddlers too!"

"I expect he could catch them," said Zek. There was nothing Hezekiah considered beyond the reach of Hector's intelligence and ability. Hector was actually still a puppy. He was a Christmas gift begged from Hezekiah's parents and acquired from Mr Straw's farm. Hector was clumsy, hyperactive, usually unpredictable, always verging on excited, and he adored his young master with lavish, unsparing devotion. He was mostly white and often dirty. Mr Straw wasn't exactly sure what type of dog he was; he appeared to be a mix of all the types of dogs in Aletheia. But it didn't matter to Zek what Hector was; he was certain he had all the best characteristics a dog could possibly have.

"Have you seen a Meddler in Aletheia?" Zek asked Mrs De Voté.

Mrs De Voté nodded. "Just the other day," she said. "Only a street or two away from here!"

"That's very serious, isn't it?" said Zek.

"I'm afraid it is," said Mrs De Voté. "But you can all play your part in getting rid of them!"

"Can we?" asked Zek. He wondered if the other adults thought so too. They didn't tell the kids anything; perhaps they didn't think the children of Aletheia could make that much difference.

"Meddlers hate prayer and the Bible," said Mrs De Voté. "They know those things will defeat them. Whatever happens in this wicked scheme of theirs, don't forget to keep praying and keep defending the Truth with the Word of God!"

"I won't forget," said Zek earnestly. He whistled to Hector who completely ignored him, being beside himself with excitement at the root of a new daffodil that he had, after frantic, excited labours, just uncovered. "Hector!" cried Zek in dismay, looking at the wreckage of Mrs De Voté's neat pot of spring flowers and the soil flung carelessly around the newly swept pavement. "Bad dog, Hector!"

"Never mind," said Mrs De Voté with an exasperated sigh that she tried to hide from Zek. "If God can make a donkey speak and do His will[3], perhaps even Hector can be used to defeat the plan of the Meddlers!"

Hezekiah thought about Mrs De Voté's words as he walked across the dewy fields with Hector capering happily beside him, quite oblivious to his recent disgrace. The birds were singing; the trees were showering

pink and white blossom on the lush, green grass; the sun shone from a cloudless blue sky. The countryside was washed and ironed; budding and growing and thriving; labouring to produce an abundant harvest. Nothing seemed amiss about Aletheia this morning. If the Meddlers had a plan, where was the evidence that it was a serious threat to the city?

Hezekiah approached Mr Straw's farmhouse just as Mr Straw appeared from the barn with a wheelbarrow full of manure. Mr Straw's house was, in Zek's opinion, the best house in Aletheia. Mr Straw was its architect – and it was very sturdy, and definitely curious, with no part quite the same as another. It straddled one of the many small rivers – which contained the Water of Sound Doctrine – that snaked through the Pray-Always Farmlands, watering the crops and animals, before ending in the deep, encircling boundary of water which protected the city. Mr Straw even had a big water wheel that turned with the flowing river, powering his house with light and heat. Zek couldn't imagine anything nicer than having a house built over the Water of Sound

Doctrine. And besides all this, Mr Straw lived on his own and didn't even have to wipe his boots when he went inside, or tidy away his things, or do the washing up as soon as it should be done. Zek had the suspicion his mother wouldn't entirely approve of these arrangements, but to him they were the mark of a great man.

"Hello, Mr Straw!" called Zek as soon as he was within reach.

"Ah, Zek!" said Croft Straw, spying the boy and his dog. "I wondered if you and Hector were coming today.

"I was talking to Mrs De Voté," said Zek, as explanation for being late.

"She's not been taken by the Fretters, has she?" asked Mr Straw with concern. "She's one of our best prayer warriors!"

"No," said Zek, wondering what it meant to be 'taken by the Fretters'. "At least, I don't think so. Hector messed up her flower pot though."

"Ah," said Mr Straw with a smile, bending down to pat Hector who was leaping up and down around his feet. "Well, that's not as serious as Fretters anyway!"

"Isn't it?" asked Zek, picturing the smashed spring flowers. He grabbed the spare pitchfork – the special one Mr Straw allowed him to use – and began to extract manure from the barn and add it to the now emptied barrow. Fly, Mr Straw's clever black-and-white collie dog, joined them in the barn and Hector capered around Fly in exuberant excitement. Fly deftly avoided most of Hector's licks and nibbles and boxing paws. Fly always looked at Hector in a longsuffering and mildly-pitying way, as if she knew he was slightly mad, and certainly far below her own intelligence.

"The managers in Aletheia think Fretters are responsible for the latest bout of sickness among the prayer warriors at Run-the-Race Retirement Home," explained Mr Straw, picking up a big load of dung on his pitchfork and throwing it neatly into the barrow.

Hezekiah was glad Mr Straw told him things and talked to him like a grown-up. Mr Straw was the Pray-Always Farmlands representative at the important Management Meetings held in the Academy of Soldiers-of-the-Cross. These were meetings where the chief people in the city planned the defence of Aletheia and discussed how they would overturn the Meddlers' plan. Zek thought this made Mr Straw very important.

Zek hoisted a big pitchfork of dung, after the manner of Mr Straw, and sent it spinning through the air to land all around the barrow and not on it at all. Zek patiently went to clear up the results, aided by Hector who picked up a clump and shook it very hard, sending straw and manure spinning in every direction. Hector ate some too, treating it as a great delicacy.

"He's hungry quite a lot," said Zek, anxious to excuse Hector. Then he turned to Mr Straw. "I, uh, I heard, that is, uh, people are saying that the Meddlers' plan is already working on the people in The Outskirts," he said. He was very glad when Mr Straw didn't ask him how he had heard this. He certainly didn't want to confess he had been eavesdropping on his father.

"It's true," said Mr Straw. He leaned on his pitchfork, in the entrance of his barn, and looked down the gently sloping fields all the way to where the Water of Sound Doctrine circled Aletheia and kept them all safe. Right by the boundary of the water, people had built houses. These areas were known as 'The Outskirts' and the people who lived here were exposed to greater danger because they lived away from the cross in the centre of Aletheia. Some of them could no longer see the cross from their houses; they forgot about how much the Lord Jesus had done when He died at the cross to save them from their sins[4]. And so, instead of focussing on the cross and doing things that would please the Lord Jesus, they were distracted by other things instead.

"The people in The Outskirts are already distracted from praying. The folk at Law Villas have even drawn up their own five-point prayer guide all about *how* to pray, instead of actually praying! The Chief has tried to reason with them, but they're refusing to be distracted from their campaign to get people to pray in the right way."

"Oh," said Zek, "is that what the Meddlers are trying to get people to do? Just talk about prayer, instead of praying?"

"It's certainly part of their plan," said Mr Straw grimly. "You must have heard the Meddlers' rhyme that first alerted Aletheia to the Meddlers' plan?"

Hezekiah nodded. Nearly everyone in Aletheia had heard the Meddlers' rhyme. Most people thought it was silly, and the Bible Poetry teacher at school said it was a very bad poem indeed. Zek knew it by heart and he repeated:

"Fretters for the Old,

Distractions for the Young,

Issues for the In-Betweens,

Our Plan have we begun!"

"Yes, that's it," said Mr Straw. "Well, the poem shows how the

Meddlers will target us. They've released swarms of Fretters to make the older people fret and worry and get ill and anxious about things, and generally not pray as much. They're going to be distracting you young folk somehow, perhaps through this ridiculous *revolting* Agreement of Nations. And as we've just been saying, we know they're already successfully stirring up issues for all the in-between people who are adults, so they quarrel about all kinds of issues and talk *about* praying *instead* of praying!"

"Do you think the Meddlers' attack is really going to happen?" asked Zek.

"It's already happening," said Mr Straw. "I knew there was something bad afoot when we suffered a strange blight across Pray-Always farms last summer. You young folk must be on your guard too. And you can always pray, you know, just as much as the rest of us."

Zek nodded, feeling the weight of that solemn responsibility. "Mr Mustardpot is going to talk to us all this morning," he said. "I think he might tell us all about what's happening in Aletheia."

"Then you'd best be on your way," said Mr Straw.

Zek, remembering that Mr Mustardpot did *not* approve of children who were late, left Hector pestering Fly the collie, and hurried back across the fields to school. Hector often spent the day at Mr Straw's farm, and Zek collected him after school. Fly looked reproachfully after Hezekiah's retreating figure. Now she had to put up with Hector for a whole day!

CHAPTER 2
SPECULATION

Hezekiah was only just in time to join the other children streaming into the massive school hall. They were all jumbled up, not in their usual classes, and he managed to work his way towards his older twin brother and sister, Hugo and Henrietta, and their friends. He was bursting with importance. He had something he must tell them, which he thought might even be more important than whatever Mr Mustardpot was going to announce.

"Henry!" he panted as he reached his sister's side.

"Have you been running, Zek?" she asked. "Oh! You've got dung on your shoes! I thought I could smell something! And what on earth are you holding...?"

"It's blossom," said Zek, still slightly out of breath from his frantic race to school.

"Well, I suppose I could see that it's blossom," said Henrietta wryly. "But why are you carrying it into the school hall? Don't you think it might look a bit odd?"

Zek hadn't considered how odd his branch of blossom might appear. He hadn't had time to put it somewhere safe. He had stopped and picked it for Mrs De Voté on his way to school from Mr Straw's farm.

He intended it as a gift to make up for Hector spoiling her flower pot. But that wasn't uppermost in his mind now.

"There was a Meddler in the blossom!" he exclaimed. "Henry, I saw a *real, live* Meddler!"

Henrietta Wallop didn't have time to tell her youngest brother what she thought of his claim of seeing one of the elusive, much talked about Meddlers. She deftly managed to remove Hezekiah's small branch of blossom – which was dropping its fragile white flowers all over the floor – and placed it on a nearby shelf. She loved her brother and she didn't want Zek, who could be very absentminded, to be laughed at by all the pupils for appearing at this important meeting with a branch of blossom.

"We'll talk afterwards," she whispered.

They all took their seats on the floor of the massive school hall amongst the other children. Zek was squashed between Hugo and Henrietta. Their cousin, Josie Faithful, was by them, and their good friend, Dusty Addle, was next to Hugo; seated by Dusty was Hugo's best friend, Timmy Trial, who was on a long visit to Aletheia and attended their school. Mr Mustardpot hadn't yet appeared and the children quietly speculated amongst themselves what the Headmaster was going to talk about. Some hoped Mr Mustardpot was about to announce they would get extra holidays, or that school was going to close for the rest of the year; other children thought the announcement was going to be about the Meddlers – since that was certainly what people were talking about in Aletheia; and yet others hoped they would learn about the intriguing Revolting Nations Agreement which was all the rage in the land of Err.

"I wonder if it's true that Err needs the city of Aletheia to cooperate in order to sign up to the Revolting Nations Agreement," speculated Hugo, as they all waited for Mr Mustardpot to appear. "If that *is* true, then Aletheia can actually stop Err from signing the Agreement and getting closer to Iniquitous!"

"I've never heard of Iniquitous before," said Timmy. Timmy, who lived with the Wallop family, was not actually from the land of Err; he was still new to many things about Aletheia and Err.

"It's a dreadful land," said Hugo. "I'm not exactly sure what they get up to there, but I've heard Dad say it's worse than Err – so if Err signs this Agreement-thing, then the land will get worse and definitely won't want to know the Truth of the Bible."

"I don't think you're exactly an expert on the land of Iniquitous, Hugo," observed Henrietta. Henrietta was prone to comment on Hugo's expostulations. It was part of the usual exchanges between the twins and the others were used to it.

"I've heard the Rescuers at the Academy say that every Region in a country has to be represented in order for a nation to enter the Agreement," said Dusty, getting back to the point. Since he had a Saturday job inside the Academy of Soldiers-of-the-Cross, Dusty was a very useful informant on such matters.

"Well, that would mean Err *can't* enter the Agreement without Aletheia," concluded Hugo. "After all, Aletheia is the central Region in the land of Err! I think they call us Region 15."

"Thank you, Hugo," said Henrietta. "I think we already knew that Aletheia is known as Region 15 in Err."

"I didn't know Aletheia was an official Region in Err," commented Timmy.

"Err wanted Aletheia to join the Council of Err – that's the Government," explained Josie. "So, years ago, they made Aletheia an official Region in the land, the last Region, which is why Aletheia is number 15."

"But the announcement *must* be about Meddlers," said Zek with a frown, still focussed on his all-important news. "I really *did* see one in the blossom tree, you know!"

"I wonder what *Team WondERRful* will do if Aletheia refuses to enter the Agreement," mused Josie. Team WondERRful was the name the Council of Err had given to the regional representatives who would sign the Revolting Nations Agreement.

"Revolting Nations Agreement!" said Henrietta. "I still think that name must be a joke!"

"It's pretty accurate, anyway," remarked Timmy. "It *is* revolting!"

"Except that the Agreement folk mean that it's cool to revolt and rebel against authority," said Dusty.

"Aletheia will *never* send a representative to sign an Agreement which is about making closer ties with the land of Iniquitous!" said Hugo.

"Thank you, Hugo," said Henrietta. "I think we can assume the Chief of Aletheia hasn't lost all his marbles and forgotten everything Aletheia stands for!"

"I expect the Chief already has a plan for dealing with the Team WondERRful representatives," observed Dusty, who was by nature a peacemaker and often tried to diffuse any bickering between the twins.

"The Chief is already meeting with managers and important people to discuss such things," said Hugo. "He has a lot on his mind."

"I don't think you're exactly a mind-reader, Hugo," said Henrietta.

"I thought the Management Meetings were to discuss the plan of the Meddlers to attack Aletheia," said Josie.

"I expect the Chief can think of two things at once," said Dusty peaceably.

"He's a very clever man," observed Timmy, making Josie giggle. "But perhaps the two things – the Revolting Agreement and the Meddlers – are linked in some way," he added perceptively.

"I *saw a Meddler*," said Zek, reminded once again of his momentous news by Timmy's mention of Meddlers.

"Where did you see the Meddler, Zek?" asked Dusty, leaning around the others to see him.

"In a blossom tree! It was on Pray-Always Farmlands when I was picking blossom," said Zek, pleased someone was interested in his all-consuming news.

"Why were you picking blossom, Zek?" asked Josie.

"Shhh," Hugo hissed.

Mr Philologus Mustardpot strode onto the platform.

An instant hush descended across the hall.

CHAPTER 3
MR MUSTARDPOT'S CHALLENGE

You could not miss the presence of Mr Mustardpot; and you did not dare to ignore it. He was secretly known as 'Whiskers' by the children on account of his big, bushy, alarming whiskers. But whiskers weren't the only thing that was alarming about Mr Mustardpot. He was very big, and very tall, with the most penetrating, all-seeing eyes, and a booming voice. He was in charge of education in Aletheia and made sure the schools in Aletheia only taught what the Bible said. All the children were in awe of him; none wanted to feel his disapproval.

Mr Mustardpot cleared his throat and gazed over the assembled children. Every child in the school was in the massive school hall.

Each felt he was seeing only them, searching out their blemishes and mistakes and knowing them all. Zek wondered if Mr Mustardpot could see or smell the dung on his shoes. Certainly a few kids close by wrinkled their noses and frowned at him, but Mr Mustardpot didn't look particularly disapprovingly at Zek.

"Benjamin Wright, Charlie Steady," Mr Mustardpot fixed his intimidating stare on a couple of boys somewhere in the middle of the school hall. "Please move seats so that there are at least ten people between you." There was a ripple of laughter. Benjamin and Charlie were well known pranksters. There was almost certain to be mischief wherever the two appeared together. There was some shuffling to accommodate the changes that took place, and Mr Mustardpot, evidently not finding anything else that met his immediate displeasure, waited until utter silence filled even the corners of the massive space.

"I expect you've all been wondering about Team WondERRful and the Revolting Nations Agreement," the Headmaster began without preamble.

The children stirred with interest and excitement.

"Well, I'm not going to talk about that," said Mr Mustardpot, and something like a sigh moved through the rafters of the big school hall. Many of the children thought it would be great to have an Aletheian representative for Team WondERRful and be part of an Agreement with the land of Iniquitous. It all sounded so important and exciting!

"And I dare say some of you are interested in the Meddlers too!" continued Mr Mustardpot.

"I *saw* a *Meddler*," Zek whispered to himself.

"But I'm not going to talk much about those pesky rascals either!"

boomed Mr Mustardpot. Nervous giggling rippled through the room. It was abundantly obvious that Mr Mustardpot would like to personally terrorise the wicked Meddlers until they bothered the city of Aletheia no more.

"Instead, I want you to imagine a world without prayer," said Mr Mustardpot.

The children stirred again, this time in surprise. Imagine a world without prayer...? This wasn't the important announcement they were expecting!

"Can anybody tell me what that would be like?"

The stirring ceased and every child looked steadily away from Mr Mustardpot. *No one* wanted to speak in front of the whole school. Even Flair Scholar, one of the brightest girls in the school, didn't want to answer now.

"No?" boomed Mr Mustardpot. "Anyone at all?"

Zek could see the other teachers, who were seated on the stage behind Mr Mustardpot, also stirring uneasily. They probably didn't want to be noticed either.

"Well," continued Mr Mustardpot, "perhaps you are wise not to answer. Perhaps it is beyond the realms of all our imaginations. But I tell you one thing! It is a world I would *not* want to live in!"

His voice echoed around the frozen stillness of dozens of long rows of children, and washed over the teachers who were as motionless as statues along the back of the stage.

"It is a world of no hope!" thundered Mr Mustardpot. "A world where none of us can cry to God to save us from our sins[4]! Or ask His help in times of need! Or ask God to guide and direct and take any interest in us at all! Can you imagine how terrible a world like that would be? We would all be DOOMED forever! And *that's* just what the *Meddlers* would have us to be!"

Shudders ran up and down Hezekiah's spine. The massive room echoed with the cry of DOOMED! DOOMED! DOOMED! Around the walls, up to the rafters, through the windows reverberated the awful message of DOOMED, if the world was without any means of communication with God; if there was no prayer.

"Now, most people think I shouldn't be telling you this," said Mr Mustardpot, and Zek and Hugo and Henrietta and their friends held their breath in excitement, "but I think you children, especially those of you who have trusted in the Lord Jesus and belong to Him[5], have a part to play in the defence of the city of Aletheia! For those of you who aren't yet saved from the debt you owe for all your sins, then, as always, I urge you to turn to the Lord Jesus who can set you free from your debt because He has already paid the price for your sins[6]! For those of you who are saved and already Christians, there's a verse in the Bible which applies to you. If you have faith in the power of God, even faith as small as a very small seed – the mustard seed – then you can move mountains![7]"

Hezekiah sat listening with avid attention. That meant him! That meant kids *could* do something for the defence of Aletheia, just as much as the adults! He wasn't sure why he'd want to actually move a mountain, but if faith the size of a tiny seed could do *that*, then surely it could remove the Meddlers too!

"Of course," Mr Mustardpot continued solemnly, "true faith is always based upon some command or promise of God. Don't expect to perform some spectacular stunt just to show off! But if you pray to God for things that are according to His guidance and His commands in the Bible[8], then you can have utmost confidence that mountainous difficulties will be miraculously removed and *nothing* will be impossible, even the defeat of the Meddlers and every enemy of our great God!"

Zek felt Mr Mustardpot was talking only to him. He hung on every word. He really could be a part of defeating the Meddlers! If he placed all of his confidence in God and prayed according to what the Bible said, then *anything* might happen!

"Learn the Truth of Sanctification!" said Mr Mustardpot. "See what great things God can do through people who are willing to be set apart for Him!"

"*Sanctification*," whispered Zek, wishing he had a notebook to write it down. He didn't know what it meant or even how to spell it, but if Mr Mustardpot said it was important to defeat the Meddlers, then he needed to learn exactly what it was.

"And now for the reason you are all here," said Mr Mustardpot. "I'm setting you an important assignment." There was a collective sigh, a bit like a groan, amongst the children. They hadn't expected the Headmaster's announcement to be about an assignment! Nobody really wanted extra schoolwork, except, perhaps, Flair Scholar. Flair wasn't a Christian but she studied very hard and wanted top marks for everything. She loved assignments.

"This is a special project," continued Mr Mustardpot. "And the prize for the winner is *one hundred* house points!"

There was a collective gasp and an outbreak of excitement, at which Mr Mustardpot smiled and didn't protest. One hundred house points was massive! It practically guaranteed your school house would win the trophy at the end of the year. There were three school houses – Faith, Hope and Charity; all the children worked very hard through the year to get points so that their school house might win the gold trophy.

When the noise had died down, Mr Mustardpot continued, "One hundred house points will go to the student who completes the best piece of work on the subject of 'The Importance of Sanctification and Prayer'. It can be written, drawn, practical, or anything you like. You might want to consider a visit to Sanctification on Redemption Square. You have the rest of this term to work on it."

There was plenty of fevered speculation as the children left the great hall and dispersed for their morning break. Children discussed the Meddlers, the Revolting Nations Agreement, the strange assignment, and the incredible prize of one hundred house points.

"We must discuss what we're going to do to help," Hugo said, as they pressed through the crowds of other kids.

"What do you mean?" asked Henrietta.

"How we're going to help defeat the Meddlers, of course," said Hugo. "It's important!"

"I think we all know it's important, Hugo," began Henrietta.

"I *saw* a Meddler!" interrupted Zek, struggling to get through the throngs of children, eager to be helpful in this most significant matter.

"What about the assignment?" asked Josie, thinking about the coveted prize of one hundred house points.

"Defeating the Meddlers is the most important thing," said Henrietta, eager for some action.

"Let's find somewhere quiet to talk about it," said Hugo.

"The upstairs classroom?" suggested Dusty. "I think it's still being painted."

Henrietta, Josie, Timmy and Zek followed Hugo and Dusty away from the melee of children heading out to the playgrounds for their break. They slipped down a deserted passageway. None of the teachers observed them, and they reached the top floor without being noticed. They could smell fresh paint from the empty classroom at the end of the corridor. They hastened towards their meeting place. They needed to talk and plan. For all of them felt that on them might rest the fate of Aletheia.

CHAPTER 4
FRIENDS REUNITED

For Jack Merryweather, this school day was just like any other in his ordinary life in the village of Steeple-Bumpton. He looked out of the classroom window and wondered, not for the first time, why the sun always shone the brightest on days he was on classroom duty. It had rained most of the winter, and nearly all of the spring, but at last the sun had returned, and the shouts of the other children in the playground echoed around the deserted classroom in a way which did not help him perform his duties. What made matters worse was that his friend, Alfie McPhee, who usually shared classroom duty with him, was off sick. Marigold Goody had offered to help him, but Jack, alarmed at the prospect of having to meet Marigold's conscientious standards in his efforts to water the plants, dust the shelves, sweep the floor, and empty the bin, had refused any help at all.

He returned the broom to the cupboard. He hoped no one noticed the small heaps of dust under some of the desks. He had carefully avoided leaving any under Marigold's desk. He stepped back into the classroom from the cupboard and considered the results of his labours. He was surprised how clean and fresh the classroom was. It looked as if it had been freshly painted; it even *smelled* freshly painted. In fact, the more he considered it, the more he realised it didn't look like the same classroom at all.

Jack heard voices approaching the door. He hoped Marigold Goody hadn't decided to come and help him after all. But who else – apart from Marigold – would leave their morning break and the sunshine and return to the classroom before they needed to...?

Hugo opened the spare classroom door and poked his head around it to check the room was free. "It's alright," he said to the others, "there's no one here...oh!" He stared at Jack in disbelief.

"Hugo?" ventured Jack.

"Jack?" said Hugo. "Jack! Well...!"

"Did you say *Jack?*" demanded Timmy, suddenly pushing forward.

"Jack!" cried Hezekiah, tumbling through the door, anxious to see his friend.

"It really *is* Jack!" said Dusty with a big grin, patting him on the back.

"Hi Jack," said Josie, with a wide smile.

"Jack!" cried Henrietta and gave him a big hug.

They all knew Jack Merryweather very well. He had shared adventures with all of them. He was the boy who had faced the Snares with Zek when Timmy had been taken captive[9]. He had given Dusty his blanket and gone with Timmy on a broken journey which ended in the rescue of Josie[1]. Being younger than the others, he was Hezekiah Wallop's special friend. But he was universally popular with the older kids too; they always seemed to think he knew exactly what he was doing. Jack didn't think he knew a great deal at all. He usually just went with the flow in adventures. But he did have the ability to be calm under pressure, and to simply trust in God in difficult situations.

"I might have known you would come back to help us defeat the Meddlers!" exclaimed Hugo.

"Do you have any inside information?" asked Josie.

Jack glanced at Timmy who grinned at him and shrugged. Timmy was from Jack's own village. He knew how things worked in Jack's country. "Uh, no, I don't really have any information as such," said Jack. It was not a complete surprise to him that they were talking about defeating Meddlers; Jack had been on the previous adventure when the Meddlers' wicked plan had been revealed[1].

"I expect you'll think of a good plan to defeat the Meddlers," said Hezekiah loyally. He was bursting to tell Jack all about Hector, and the Meddler he'd seen that morning, and all the things that had happened since Jack was last in Aletheia.

"We must catch up on everything," said Timmy, wanting to know plenty from Jack about life in his home village.

Jack had missed his friend Timmy. Somehow, Timmy had been

allowed to go away to school in Aletheia for a while, but how this had been arranged, and quite how Timmy came and went to Aletheia, were still a mystery to Jack. All Jack knew was that it was called 'Underground Entry'. It was something he was most intrigued about.

"Never mind about catching up just now," said Henrietta briskly. "We've got plenty of time for that later. Right now we're meeting to discuss what we're going to do to help defeat the Meddlers! We can't let them stop prayer!"

"We need a name for our group," said Josie decisively.

"Why?" asked Dusty.

"Because that's what we should do," said Josie. She was the organised one amongst them all. She had a pen and a pad open even now, and was preparing to record notes about exactly what they were going to do.

"Shouldn't we decide what, uh, what we're doing first?" asked Timmy.

"Yes," said Hugo.

Josie rolled her eyes. "We're going to be part of the defence of Aletheia," she said, as if this was abundantly obvious. "We're going to pray and plan, and learn how to defeat the Meddlers! That's more important than the assignment – even if it does mean winning one hundred house points! I'm sure we all agree about that!"

"I really wanted Faith House to win the trophy this year," sighed Henrietta regretfully, but she didn't disagree with Josie.

"You always want Faith House to win it, Henry," Zek reminded her.

"I expect Hope will win it again," said Henrietta.

"Alright," said Hugo, taking charge. "I think we're all agreed on this, aren't we? We mustn't mind about the one hundred house points and the Sanctification and Prayer assignment. We know there's a problem with the Meddlers attacking Aletheia and trying to stop prayer. So, do we all agree we've got to be part of the defence and *do* something?"

"Jo just said that in a lot less words," said Henrietta.

"In fewer words," murmured Dusty, who liked to be precise.

"I'm sure we're all agreed," said Timmy quickly, wanting to get on with the important business of the meeting.

"I *saw* a Meddler this very morning!" said Zek.

"Yes, OK Zek," said Hugo kindly.

"Who's going to be the leader?" asked Henrietta.

"I think it should be Hugo," said Dusty.

"Or Timmy," said Josie.

"Hugo," said Timmy.

"If you're sure," said Hugo.

"What about Henry?" asked Zek, who was very loyal to his sister and saw the downcast expression on her face.

"Thank you, Zek," said Henrietta with dignity.

There was a fleeting silence which wasn't reassuring to Henrietta's prospects of leadership.

"Do we need to vote?" asked Hugo.

"No," said Henrietta with as much remaining dignity as she could muster.

"You're good at other things, Henry," said Josie.

"Thanks, Jo," said Henrietta.

"Lots of things," said Dusty encouragingly. He secretly admired Henrietta very much and didn't like to see her disappointed. He wondered if he should have been so quick to nominate Hugo.

"Let's call ourselves the Mustardseeds," said Zek.

CHAPTER 5
THE MUSTARDSEEDS

"The Mustardseeds," said Hugo thoughtfully. "You know, I think you've hit the nail on the head, Zek!"

Hezekiah went red with pleasure and Jack whispered "Good one, Zek!" in his friend's ear.

"Well done, Zek!" said Henrietta. "The Mustardseeds has my vote!"

"It's a good name because it will remind us to have faith in God, even if it's only small faith, like a small mustard seed[7]. If we place all our faith and confidence in God and believe He can do the things He says in the Bible, then we can do great things, like Mr Mustardpot said!" explained Hugo.

"I think we all heard Mr Mustardpot say that, Hugo," said Henrietta, who was still smarting that Hugo had been so easily elected leader when she hadn't been considered at all.

"I also thought of the name of the Mustardseeds because it's sort of like Mr Mustardpot's name," said Zek. "It's like we're helping him too."

"That's so sweet, Zek," said Josie.

Hezekiah certainly hadn't intended to be *sweet*; Jack and he exchanged understanding grimaces.

"Now, we must nominate tasks," said Hugo decisively. "Jo, can you write this down?"

"Righty-ho," said Josie willingly.

"I don't see why a *girl* has to do all the writing," said Henrietta.

"I didn't exactly say a *girl* had to do all the writing, Henry," said Hugo. "I only asked Jo..."

"It's fine," said Josie quickly. "I like doing notes." She grinned at the others. They were all used to the twins bickering and everyone knew that deep down they were fiercely loyal and protective of each other.

"As long as girls get to do *interesting* things too," said Henrietta in an undertone.

Hugo rolled his eyes when Henrietta wasn't looking. "Now, let's decide what each of us is going to do," he said.

Jack couldn't think what he would do; he wasn't sure he was particularly good at anything. Hezekiah was quite prepared however. He was thinking of Hector and all the things his beloved dog could help them achieve. Like Mrs De Voté said, God could use dogs if He wanted to.

"I can scout out the city, gather intelligence, and generally coordinate and lead our missions," said Hugo.

"That doesn't actually mean anything at all," said Henrietta. "*I* could do all of that too!"

"Henry, you're good at talking to people and getting information from them," said Josie.

"Well..." said Henrietta

"Uh, I can provide information from the Central Control Room," offered Dusty.

"Excellent!" said Hugo. Dusty spent all of his spare hours outside of school working at the Central Control Room in the Academy of Soldiers-of-the-Cross. Just about everything that happened in Aletheia, and in the wider land of Err too, passed through the Control Room. Dusty was quickly becoming trusted with ever-increasing responsibilities, especially since so many Rescuers and other support staff were now busy elsewhere in Err.

"I think Dusty has the most important job of any of us," said Timmy. "I'm not sure what I can do..."

"You'll be very useful identifying and knowing about Meddlers," said Josie briskly, writing it down. "After all, you, me, and Jack have the most experience of being attacked by Meddlers!"

Jack was suddenly very glad he had once been attacked by Meddlers[1]. It meant he could help the Mustardseeds now.

"What about the thing Mr Mustardpot mentioned called Sanctification?" asked Zek, but nobody paid much attention.

"And you're my second-in-command too, Timmy," said Hugo. "We'll scout out the city together."

"What about Dusty?" asked Henrietta indignantly.

"I'm fine," said Dusty with a grin. "I'm better concentrating on the Control Room side of things!"

"Precisely," said Hugo, giving his exasperating twin a stern glance.

"I've got Hector!" Zek burst out at last.

Josie laughed. "Noted that Hector is also a member of the Mustardseeds," she said.

"Uh, I'm not exactly sure Hector will be..." Hugo began uncertainly. They all knew how much Zek loved his dog, and none of them wanted to upset him by pointing out that, more than anything, Hector was likely to be a big nuisance with his invariably dirty paws, frantic, chaotic activity, and yaps and barks at the smallest, oddest things. "Perhaps when he's trained..."

"Nonsense!" said Henrietta, catching the expression on Zek's face. "You could train him to catch Meddlers!" she added brightly.

"Really, Henry, you shouldn't encourage him," muttered Hugo.

"But that's what Mrs De Voté said!" exclaimed Hezekiah. "She said God could use anything, even a dog!"

"Well, we'll see, alright?" said Hugo.

Hezekiah knew they didn't think Hector could do much. While the others talked about tasks and Josie scribbled notes, he whispered in Jack's ear and told him all about Hector, and Mr Straw, and the fact that Zek still wore Jack's old spy watch which he had loaned him, and all the other things he thought his friend should know.

"Alright," said Josie at last. "Is everybody listening? I'm going to read out the list of tasks we have agreed to do before our next meeting."

Jack and Zek paid attention once more.

"Hugo, you and Timmy will start to scout out the city and The Outskirts and ask people if they're praying enough. And if they're not praying, then find out why. Like carrying out a survey."

"Agreed," said Hugo.

"Dusty, you are our official intelligence gatherer about what's happening in Err and the strength of the defence of Aletheia – prayer power, Meddler presence, and so on."

"Aye, aye!" said Dusty cheerfully.

"I'm going to write up our notes, plan our meeting agendas..."

"As agreed with me," Hugo interrupted.

"...and Henry and I will visit Miss Candour Communique of *The Truth* newspaper to find out more about the problems in Aletheia," concluded Josie.

They all looked at the two younger boys, Jack and Hezekiah, who sat together on the fringes of the group.

"We're going to hunt Meddlers and Fretters with Hector!" Zek declared boldly.

The others laughed, although not unkindly.

"And I will get information from Mr Straw about the adults' meetings at the Academy," added Zek.

Hugo was clearly doubtful. "I don't know that Mr Straw can tell us anything that Dusty won't be able to find out," he said. "But you find out what you can and let us know!"

Hezekiah knew the others didn't think he and Jack could do much. He was glad it only took faith the size of a mustard seed for God to work. It meant that, no matter what the older Mustardseeds thought, he and Jack could do great things for the defence of Aletheia too.

The Mustardseeds had barely finished their meeting, which had ended in them remembering to pray about all the things they were going to do before their next meeting, when there was a knock on the door.

"Come in," said Hugo, assuming responsibility for welcoming the intruder and hoping it wasn't a teacher.

To their surprise, Flair Scholar poked her head around the door. She was her usual untidy self: utterly unconcerned about her personal appearance in her quest to be the best at everything academic. She paid no attention whatsoever to the combination of clothes she put on in the morning; one day she had even come to school in her slippers. She had tangled dark hair which always needed brushing. She wore glasses which made her eyes seem unusually large and which were smeared so badly no one knew how she could see through them at all. As usual she had a large satchel of books slung around her. She was always reading books.

"Did I miss the meeting?" she asked earnestly.

There was stunned silence amongst the Mustardseeds.

"Uh, I don't think..." Hugo began, utterly bewildered.

"But you weren't asked to the meeting," said Henrietta bluntly.

"We're the Mustardseeds, you see," said Zek, and then wondered if he shouldn't have said that. After all, perhaps they were meant to be a secret.

"I wanted to join you," said Flair, "to talk about winning the assignment."

"Assignment?" said Dusty. "What assignment?"

Flair smiled as if she knew they were only teasing her. "You're talking about winning one hundred house points for the Importance of Sanctification and Prayer assignment, right?" she said. She thought that the looks of blank surprise that she received were surprisingly real. "If you could help me to win it, I would ask Mr Mustardpot if some points could go to your school houses too. I don't think you're in Hope House, are you?" Flair paused, puzzled at the stunned silence around her. "Look, I just thought you could help me with information about prayer from a, uh, Christian perspective, you see? It's not a big deal!"

Another bewildered silence greeted Flair's announcement.

"I thought Christians were meant to be kind," she said in a hurt voice.

"But we weren't talking about winning the house points!" said Henrietta. "We're only interested in stopping the plan of the Meddlers to attack prayer and hurt Aletheia!"

Flair looked around at all the Mustardseeds. She seemed astonished that Henrietta meant what she said. "You don't want to win one hundred points for your school house?!" she asked.

"Of course we do," said Henrietta, who really did want to win the house trophy.

"I don't think we've got time to concentrate on Mr Mustardpot's assignment," explained Hugo, "except, perhaps, as a practical assignment! We want to do something *real* to help Aletheia."

Flair shrugged. She wasn't a Christian. She didn't take any Bible teaching personally at all. She only wanted to do the best assignment so she had top marks and won the coveted house trophy for Hope House. "Well," she said, "if you don't mind, could I just observe everything you do? I'll take notes and such. It really might help me win the Importance of Prayer assignment!"

"Well," said Hugo, "I think that would be alright, wouldn't it?" He looked at Timmy, his second-in-command.

"Alright with me," said Timmy.

Flair smiled brightly at Timmy. There was vague, tacit agreement from around the room. No one really knew what else to do.

"But no interfering, and no telling anyone else," said Hugo.

Flair looked solemnly around the Mustardseeds. "I promise," she said.

CHAPTER 6
KNOW YOUR ENEMY

After school, during which Jack sat in Hezekiah's classes, with only the occasional query from teachers who were obviously used to 'visiting students', Jack and Zek set off across the Pray-Always Farmlands to collect Hector and talk to Mr Straw. Jack had found the whole day very intriguing; it was amazing to be in a school where all of the subjects were to do with the Bible.

Jack, who had always wanted a dog of his own, was looking forward to meeting Hector. He wasn't quite sure what to expect. Zek had described Hector in the most glowing terms, so he was somewhat surprised at the comical appearance of the small, dirty-white, scruffy puppy, flying through the fields to meet them. But Zek was right on at least one point: there was no other dog like him in Aletheia.

"You can share him while you're here," said Zek.

"Thanks," said Jack. He tried to pat Hector while the small dog frolicked around, and Fly, Mr Straw's collie, sidled up to Jack and licked his hand.

Mr Straw made lemonade for the boys in his cluttered kitchen. He was very pleased to meet Jack – the boy who had faced the Snares with Hezekiah.

"Mr Straw," Zek said solemnly, "I saw a Meddler today!"

"Did you?"

Hezekiah nodded. "It was definitely a Meddler," he said. "I described it to Jack and he agrees, and Jack has actually been attacked by Meddlers[1], so he should know!"

"Attacked by Meddlers?" said Mr Straw, looking at Jack. "First Snares, and Meddlers too! You've certainly had your adventures, young man!"

"Things just happen," said Jack. He stroked Fly's velvet-soft ears and she pressed closer against his chair. Jack liked the big, serious collie who was trying her best to ignore Hector's sudden, impulsive nips at her feet.

Mr Straw chuckled at Jack's characteristic understatement. Then, "Tell me about the Meddler you saw," he said to Zek.

"It was in a blossom tree," said Zek.

Mr Straw looked surprised and suddenly more serious. "In the blossom?" he said. "You're quite sure?"

Hezekiah nodded. "I was picking blossom for Mrs De Voté," he said.

"Oh! I forgot it!" He suddenly remembered that his branch of blossom was still at school and probably withered. He had intended it as a gift-cum-apology for Mrs De Voté – for Hector wrecking her pot of spring flowers. "Well, anyway," he continued, "I was very close to the blossom, taking a piece, and I saw a wrinkled, cross, tiny face scowling at me! I really did!"

"Was the Meddler wearing a coloured jacket?" asked Mr Straw.

Jack knew why Mr Straw asked that. Meddlers often belonged to certain groups and specialised in all types of wicked mischief. Jack had already come across the Red-Jacket Meddlers, who were Meddlers of Doubt and Despair, and the Yellow-Jacket Meddlers, who were Meddlers of Strife.

"I think it had a bright green jacket," said Zek, wrinkling his nose and concentrating on remembering. "Yes, that was it! A bright green jacket! It wasn't quite the same green as the leaves, you see, and you could see it against the white blossom."

Mr Straw suddenly looked very solemn indeed.

"What are Green-Jacket Meddlers?" asked Jack. "I've never seen one before."

"They're Meddlers of Blight," said Mr Straw. "They'll be trying to attack our blossom and perhaps our early crops too – spreading their blight-goo on all the new buds and leaves. Then there won't be enough safe Pray-Always Farmlands food for Aletheia. And if we eat food from Err...well, that's very bad news, boys, very bad indeed!"

Neither of the two boys knew what to suggest that would be helpful. Zek looked fondly at Hector who was shaking a tea-towel on the floor. "I'm going to teach Hector to catch Meddlers," said Zek, which was the only thing he could think to bring comfort at that moment.

Jack privately thought that Fly, the collie, who was watching Hector despairingly, had a far better chance of learning to catch Meddlers.

"I must tell the Management Meeting about the Green-Jacket," murmured Mr Straw. "They'll have to know. I'll have to speak up at the meeting. We must get more prayer cover before the blight is too bad and ruins our crops!"

"What can we do to help?" asked Jack, feeling very sorry for the big famer who looked so solemn at the thought of the Meddlers at work amongst his lovely new crops.

"Pray," said Mr Straw. "You boys can always pray."

"Mr Mustardpot said that if we have faith the size of a tiny mustard seed, we can see God do wonderful things," said Zek.

"Quite right!" said Mr Straw.

"We want to do more, though," said Zek.

"For the Mustardseeds," said Jack.

"That's us," added Zek.

"Of course it is," said Mr Straw.

One of the things Zek liked most about his friend, Mr Straw, was that he didn't ask too many questions and always seemed to understand exactly what he, Zek, was talking about.

"Well, how can me and Jack and Hector do something *real* about the Meddlers?" asked Zek, quite sure that Mr Straw had all the answers.

"Praying *is* real," said Mr Straw.

"I know," said Zek. "But something else too; something to report to the Mustardseeds at the next meeting."

"Ah," said Mr Straw. "Well, I reckon the place to start, is to know your enemy!"

"Know your enemy," repeated Zek slowly.

"You mean, find out lots about the Meddlers and Fretters," said Jack.

"Exactly," said Mr Straw.

"Are there books about Meddlers and Fretters?" asked Zek.

"I reckon there must be," said Mr Straw. "The most learned people in Aletheia are the Judges. Why don't you start there?"

"The Judges' Academy!" said Zek. "My cousin, Jude Faithful, is a Junior Justice there! We'll ask him to help us."

"That sounds like just the plan," said Mr Straw.

Jack was warmly welcomed back to Foundation-of-Faith Apartments by the whole Wallop family. Mrs Daisy Wallop, Zek's mother, gave him a big hug and told him he didn't come to stay often enough. Timmy was also lodging with the Wallops. He shared Hugo's room, and Jack settled back into the spare bed in Hezekiah's room as if he had never been away. It might have been surprising to Jack, had he been of a mind to question things, that the Wallops so readily accepted him into their family and asked so few questions regarding his sudden appearance. But unexpected visitors seemed the normal state of affairs in Aletheia; there was nothing as easy as appearing when least expected and becoming part of family life there.

But it was obvious, even to Jack, who did not view things in an anxious light, that Mr and Mrs Wallop were worried. Mrs Wallop spoke in a hushed voice on the Mission Link and sighed much more than she had in the past. And Mr Wallop read *The Truth* newspaper with a frown of concern, not enjoyment.

The rest of the Mustardseeds were also interested in *The Truth* newspaper once Mr Wallop had finished reading it. Henrietta got first shot at it. "I need to read it because I'm preparing for my interview with Miss Communique," she said.

Jack and Zek were the last to pore over the Aletheian newspaper. There wasn't a great deal, as far as they could see, that was new.

They were already convinced that there were Meddlers abroad, so it was no surprise to them that there had been no fewer than *ten* sightings reported by Aletheians in the last week. One of the reports even mentioned a *Green-Jacket* Meddler, and Jack and Zek felt very knowledgeable and wise about that part. They already knew that this was a Meddler of Blight. They both looked closely at the picture of a Meddler in the newspaper. Jack felt he would never forget the wicked features of the cross, ugly, cruel flying imps that had attacked him and Timmy. But he examined the Meddler closely anyway. As Mr Straw said, they had to know their enemy.

CHAPTER 7
THE JUDGES' ACADEMY

Jack and Zek wasted no time in learning more about Meddlers and Fretters. They arranged to meet Zek's cousin, Jude Faithful, at the Judges' Academy the following afternoon, which was a half day from school. Mr Mustardpot had, in addition to setting them the Importance of Sanctification and Prayer assignment, instructed his teachers to allow the children 'study time' for this work. Jack and Zek considered that their research at the Judges' Academy exactly fitted this study time. It was, after all, connected to defeating the Meddlers' nefarious schemes. So, when Henrietta and Josie set off for their interview with Miss Candour Communique, and Hugo and Timmy set off for The Outskirts to begin their research, and Dusty went to his beloved Control Room to check the Prayer Power Monitor there, Zek and Jack and Hector set off to the Judges' Academy to see Jude Faithful.

The Judges' Academy was probably the grandest building in Aletheia. It was multi-layered, multi-pillared, grand, ornate stone and brick, and even had bits of gold on the pillars and around the windows that glinted in the sunshine. When the two boys stood at the front entrance, before huge stone pillars, Jack had considerable doubts that

Hector's presence would go unnoticed. Fly, Mr Straw's collie, might have walked obediently and quietly through the grand corridors which were undoubtedly within. But Hector...? At least Zek had the foresight to bring a lead which Hector, unused to such restraint, was biting and pulling and generally enjoying resisting and attacking. When the tall figure of Jude Faithful appeared through the pillars, he looked amused – but dubious – at the small, scruffy figure of Hector.

"Uh, sorry, Zek," he said, when he had been introduced to Jack and greeted the boys. "I should have said. I'm afraid I don't think Hector will be allowed in the Judges' Academy."

Zek frowned disapprovingly at the grand arches before them. "Are you sure?" he asked anxiously. "Does it actually say *exactly* that in the rules?"

Jude Faithful considered that and suddenly grinned. "Not *exactly*," he said, "but if we bump into Chief Judge Steady, well, I don't know if she will approve!"

Miss Sagacia Steady was the Chief Judge of Aletheia. She was a neat and tidy, serious-minded lady who was in charge of law and order in Aletheia, and, as much as possible, across the land of Err too. All the Senior Judges reported to her, and under them were Advocates, Mediators, Justices – all the way down to Junior Justices. Jude was a Junior Justice and he certainly didn't want to be noticed by Chief Judge Steady in the unpredictable presence of Hector.

But, on the other hand, he was extremely fond of his youngest cousin. Zek was very amusing and had the most original turn of mind. And the 'project' the two boys had called him about certainly brightened up an otherwise anxious, difficult day. Like everyone else in Aletheia, the staff at the Judges' Academy felt the effects of increased Fretters and low prayer power.

Zek had confided to Jack that, of all his many cousins across Aletheia, he liked Jude the most. Bourne Faithful was, of course, the hero whom everyone admired; but Jude was kind to him, laughed at his jokes, and was, in Zek's opinion, the cleverest and nicest of them all.

"Hector will have to be very good," Jude said at last, eyeing the small dog where he was 'worrying' the lead by biting it and shaking it as hard as he could. It might be rather amusing, thought Jude, to take mad, harum-scarum Hector into the quiet stillness of the Judges' Academy.

"Oh, he will be good," said Zek. "It's just that he hasn't learned everything yet."

"Hasn't he?" asked Jude. "I'd never have guessed!"

Jack laughed. He knew Jude was joking.

"Are we going to the library?" asked Zek.

"Well," said Jude, "I think that Hector's personality might be, uh, a bit too obvious there. I'm not sure Miss Bookish, the Librarian, could handle his, uh, many talents. So I'll fetch some books about Meddlers and Fretters and take them to my office instead."

They began their journey into the entry of the Judges' Academy and down a wide, spotless, white-tiled corridor. Jude began to enjoy this break in his working day. Usually the kids in Aletheia wanted to see the Academy of Soldiers-of-the-Cross, not the more serious Judges' Academy. They seldom had children visiting here. And the addition of Hector, who was very excited by absolutely everything he saw, was variety he didn't usually expect in his line of work. It would all be alright if...

Footsteps were walking briskly down the tiled corridor around the corner, coming towards them. Any moment someone would turn the corner and discover two boys and the capering Hector who had just leapt into a large urn of carefully tended flowering plants! And, as if that wasn't bad enough, Jude heard the distinct voice he was certain belonged to the *Chief Judge herself*. He had seldom seen this important lady, and he was about to walk right into her in company with two small boys and one very naughty dog.

But there were no handy doorways, nowhere to hide, and Zek, who was trying to pull Hector away from the soil in the large urn, wasn't exactly doing it quietly.

"Down, Hector!" he said sternly. "Bad boy! Down!"

Soil was spread around lavishly when Hector was, at last, removed. He yapped excitedly, a large, green leaf hanging from his mouth. And suddenly there was Chief Judge Steady, accompanied by two sedate, senior Judges, looking amazed at the sight of Hector, the two boys, and Junior Justice, Jude Faithful.

Judge Steady was certainly a person of impressive appearance. She was dressed in a long flowing robe with high heels and a white, frilly blouse. She had neat, grey hair pulled back in an excessively tidy bun. She had small sparkly glasses perched on the end of her nose. She was immaculate.

"Well, I never!" Judge Steady exclaimed in surprise. "I wondered whoever 'Hector' might be when I heard him being reprimanded! You have visitors, Faithful, is it?"

"Jude Faithful, ma'am," said Jude.

"In company with...?"

"With my cousin and his friend, and, uh, Hector the dog, ma'am. They've come to do some research."

"Hector looks very interested in researching soil and plants," remarked Judge Steady. But then the most remarkable thing happened. Careless of her high heels and long robe and spotless white blouse, Sagacia Steady got down on the floor beside Hector. "Good boy!"

she said, and Hector leapt all over her and licked her face. "Who's a gorgeous boy?!" she said in a strangely childish voice, ruffling his ears and actually *kissing his nose.* "Who's a lovely, lovely boy come to see us today, eh? Who's such a gorgeous, gorgeous boy?!"

Zek was sincerely glad the remarks were not directed at him, but Hector didn't seem to mind them. He leapt and capered and licked and whined as if Miss Steady had always been his best friend; he had no respect for Chief Judge's regal robes and high heels. And Jude, astonished and relieved, was extremely glad that Judge Steady happened to like small, scruffy dogs.

"What are you researching, boys?" asked the Judge, when she reluctantly extracted herself from Hector's exuberance, decidedly the worse for the encounter. She had two distinctly doggy-looking prints on her spotless white blouse.

"We're researching Meddlers and Fretters, ma'am," said Jack. He thought it polite to address her as Jude did; actually, he wondered if he should bow. But after Judge Steady's performance with Hector, somehow she didn't seem quite as scary and formal and important.

"We're going to teach Hector how to catch Meddlers and Fretters," added Zek earnestly.

"I see," said Judge Steady. "I heard Philologus had set his students a project. I didn't know it involved catching Meddlers!"

"It's not exactly to do with that," said Zek, who was always literal and honest. "It's actually because we're the Mustardseeds."

"Is it indeed?" asked Judge Steady solemnly. "Well, well, keep up the good work!" And the Chief Judge clattered away, with the two senior Judges following in utter bewilderment behind her.

"Do you think we should have told her about Hector's paw prints being on her?" asked Jack, as they all watched the entourage recede into the distance.

"I don't think that's necessary," said Jude drolly.

Zek was the least surprised at the encounter with the Chief Judge. It was nothing astonishing to him that people loved Hector; he positively expected it. "I knew they would like dogs here," he said.

"And, by the way, what exactly are the Mustardseeds?" asked Jude as he led them onwards into the Academy. "Anything I should know about?"

"They're us," said Zek.

"And some others," added Jack.

"Are they really?" said Jude.

"We're secret," said Zek.

"Not so secret," said Jude. "You just told the Chief Judge!"

"Perhaps I shouldn't have said," said Zek. "It sort of just came out!"

"Sometimes things do that," said Jude solemnly.

"Never mind, Zek," said Jack. "When we catch a Meddler, they'll all have to know who we are, won't they?"

Jude smiled at the small representation of the Mustardseeds he was escorting to carry out important research. "I dare say they shall," he said.

CHAPTER 8
MISS CANDOUR COMMUNIQUE

The same free afternoon that Zek and Jack went to the Judges' Academy, Henrietta and Josie set off for the offices of *The Truth* newspaper to talk to Miss Candour Communique, the Chief Editor. The newspaper offices were located on a picturesque side street in central Aletheia, the kind of place you would never come across unless you deliberately intended it. In fact, neither of the two girls, who had lived in Aletheia their whole lives, had ever visited the building of the official Aletheia newspaper. *The Truth* offices were inside a tower which stuck up above most of the crooked rooftops around, and blocked the far end of the road, its solid stone walls joining the two sides of the street, as if it were protecting them with outstretched arms. A flag displaying the words '*The Truth*' was flying from the highest point of the tower.

Miss Communique's office was on the top floor of the tower. A smartly dressed girl from the reception checked the appointment diary and then led Henrietta and Josie round and round the winding stairs to the very top of the building. They could hear clickety-clack sounds from the printing press in the basement, and tap-tap-tapping sounds, and a whirring and a buzzing too. They could not imagine what most

of the sounds were, but there was certainly an air of importance and busyness all around them. In fact, never in the history of the circulation of *The Truth* newspaper had so many copies been selling in Aletheia and even beyond. These days *everybody* wanted to know what was happening in Aletheia.

The two cousins had strikingly different approaches to the interview that Miss Communique had kindly granted them. Josie had written down questions in an orderly list and carried her neat pad, a box of pens and pencils, and the latest copy of *The Truth* that she had borrowed from her father, all in her school satchel. Henrietta had nothing at all. She had it all in her head, she said, and, after some debate on the matter, Henrietta had reluctantly agreed that Josie could lead the interview and she would "chip in when she wanted to."

"Good morning, girls," Candour Communique said cheerfully when she looked up to find the two schoolgirls in the doorway of her office. "Come on in. Nice and prompt too! Always a good start. Thank you, Violet," she added to the girl from the reception. "Perhaps you could bring us some tea? It looks like we have some thirsty work ahead!" She gestured to two chairs close to her desk and Josie sat down and opened her pad expectantly. Henrietta walked to the window and glanced into the street below.

"Just as I thought!" she exclaimed. "You can see into Redemption Square from here, right to the cross!"

"Of course," said Candour. "It keeps me focussed!"

"Henry!" hissed Josie. She was noticing the mounds of work that clearly awaited the busy Editor. It would not do for them to waste precious interview time on chit-chat.

"Oh, sorry!" said Henrietta. She scooted across the room and sat in the vacant chair.

"Right," said Candour briskly. "What can I do for you? Is this to do with the Sanctification and Prayer assignment I understand Philologus has set the school?"

"Well, not exactly," said Josie.

Candour raised her eyebrows. She knew, as did all the management team that met at the Academy of Soldiers-of-the-Cross, that Mr Mustardpot's strategy with his students was to point them to the Truth, instead of discussing Meddlers and the Revolting Nations Agreement that was such a big deal in the land of Err. She also knew the students had been allowed time off to pursue the Importance of Sanctification and Prayer project. If the students learned the Truth of Sanctification, they would be set apart and protected from the distractions of Err. She had just assumed she had been asked for an interview in connection with this work.

"It's not *directly* related," Henrietta amended. "But it *is* to do with prayer and helping Aletheia. It's just that we're doing our own thing. Our own project."

"Most intriguing," said Candour. She had a twinkle in her eyes and Josie wished she could digress from the interview to ask her where she had got her smart suit from. Candour Communique was not particularly well known by either of the girls. They only knew she was the youngest Editor of *The Truth* for some years, and that she looked very nice whenever they glimpsed her at the meetings by the cross or busy with her work about Aletheia.

"You see, we really want to help defend Aletheia against the plan

of the Meddlers, so we've formed our own group," explained Josie. "And Henry and I are responsible for finding out more about the problems in Aletheia and what the Meddlers are doing to prayer."

"I see," said Candour thoughtfully. "Does your group have a name?"

"We're called the Mustardseeds," said Henrietta promptly.

"I think," said Josie more hesitantly, "that bit might be meant to be a secret."

"Well, even newspaper Editors can keep secrets," said Candour. "I promise you won't be on the front pages of *The Truth*! And now, what are your questions?"

Josie scrutinised her pad and Henrietta was secretly glad her cousin had, after all, been organised for the interview. She felt that, had she been leading the interview, she might want to ask Miss Communique what it felt like to be an important newspaper Editor, and what she did all day at the top of the tower, and how many interesting stories she was pursuing, what secret things she had contained in her files, and all kinds of other things that wouldn't tell them anything about Aletheia and the plan of the Meddlers at all. Henrietta wanted to just look around the office, and read the interesting things framed on the walls. From what she could see they all appeared to be verses from the Bible about truth. The one in the centre, with the sunlight glinting on the gold-edged frame, read:

'O Lord, let Your lovingkindness and YOUR TRUTH continually preserve me.'[10]

Josie, meanwhile, began the interview. "We read, in the most recent edition of *The Truth...*" she began, lifting the copy of the paper she had brought with her to show Miss Communique, "...we read that there have been 'no fewer than *ten* sightings of Meddlers reported in Aletheia in the last week.' Do you think this is representative of far more Meddlers that haven't been seen?"

"Yes," said Candour directly. "I think this is just the tip of the iceberg. Prayer power is down and Meddlers have taken advantage of that and come into the city by stealth. They're quite clever at hiding, and, as at least *some* of them, if not *most* of them, are likely to be Green-Jackets, they will be hard to spot when everything around is turning green in the spring."

Josie nodded and scribbled frantically on her pad.

"What do Green-Jacket Meddlers stand for?" asked Henrietta. She noticed this was the next question in Josie's list and so far was sticking to her cousin's script.

"They are the Meddlers of Blight," said Candour. "They primarily affect fruit and crops and can even spread disease among livestock on the farms."

"Do you think the Meddlers are directing their attack on food supplies?" asked Josie.

"That's what *I* think," said Candour. "All of the reports so far mention Green-Jackets, but unfortunately I have no direct information that this is a serious part of the Meddlers' plan to undermine Aletheia. And we can't direct our precious, limited resources and prayer power where we can't prove there is a problem. There's barely enough to cover essential services as it is."

Henrietta and Josie were surprised how direct and forthcoming Miss Communique was. They had feared they would receive evasive answers that didn't really say anything at all – the kind that grown-ups were sometimes very good at. Instead, Miss Communique seemed to want them to know.

The girl from reception returned with a neat tray of tea and biscuits. Both girls felt very important to be drinking tea in Miss Communique's office, as if they were really and truly part of official business.

"What sort of information would you need to prove the Green-Jacket Meddlers mean to target Aletheian food and supplies?" asked Henrietta eagerly, as Candour poured the tea.

"I would need substantiated reports of Green-Jacket Meddlers, for example, numbers of Meddlers, and when and where they have been seen, but particularly useful would be any evidence of blight – to show they have already been at work."

"Do you think they might have started spreading blight already?" asked Josie, carefully placing her dainty teacup back on the desk while she resumed her notes.

"I wouldn't be at all surprised," said Candour. "And that would prove, beyond all reasonable doubt, that ruining the Pray-Always food supplies is part of the Meddlers' strategy."

"That's pretty serious, isn't it?" asked Henrietta.

"Can you imagine the consequences?" said Candour.

"Not enough safe food from Pray-Always Farmlands for the Christians in Aletheia," said Josie slowly.

Candour nodded. "Can you imagine how it might weaken our hold on the Truth in Aletheia if we don't have our own food and we have to eat unsafe food grown in the polluted land of Err and watered from sources such as the River Self or the River Mee?"

"The Meddlers want to weaken us, don't they?" asked Henrietta.

"Are they getting ready for a bigger attack?" asked Josie. "I know they called this plan *Phase One*, and if this is Phase One..."

"Then there's more to follow," concluded Candour. "Yes, I agree. There are many of us who feel this initial plan of distraction and attacking prayer and supplies is merely to weaken us, so that we can't defend ourselves when the real attack comes!"

The two girls forgot the list of questions and sat for a moment in silence as they considered Miss Communique's words. They didn't doubt her. As sure as they were sitting there, they knew that this was what the praying, thinking adults were worried about; and why the important meetings took place in the Academy. The Meddlers simply *had* to be stopped before they ruined the food supply and weakened the city so much that it couldn't defend itself against whatever other wickedness was planned!

"What can we do?" asked Henrietta. Her cup of tea lay forgotten; her biscuit from 'Auntie Jolly's Bakery', whose ingredients were all safely from Pray-Always Farmlands, was half-eaten and also forgotten.

How long would they even have delicious, crunchy biscuits that were safe to eat in Aletheia?

"Pray," said Candour, looking kindly at the two girls. "And don't be distracted by the Revolting Nations Agreement that Err so badly wants to sign. The spotlight will be on Aletheia because we're standing against it. But remember, even the Agreement could be part of the Meddlers' plan!"

Josie and Henrietta and the other Mustardseeds had been too busy with their own agenda to take much notice of the Agreement the land of Err was desperate to sign. Josie scribbled a note about it on her pad.

"Would it be a good idea to talk to one of the farmers about the blight the Meddlers might be spreading?" asked Henrietta. She had the look of one of her sudden ideas about her, and Josie, who was wondering about the Revolting Nations Agreement and how this might be linked to the Meddlers' plan, watched her cousin warily.

"Are you thinking of Mr Straw?" asked Josie. "Zek's friend?"

"Exactly!" said Henrietta.

"Mr Croft Straw?" asked Candour with amusement. "He isn't one of the, uh, Mustardseeds by any chance, is he?"

"Not exactly," said Henrietta. "But he's a friend of ours."

"He doesn't enjoy talking very much," said Candour, still seeming amused. "But if you can convince him to talk to me about blight on the farmlands, I will be very grateful!"

"Consider it done!" said Henrietta impulsively.

"Henry!" hissed Josie. "We don't know if Mr Straw…"

"Is there anything else you think we should be doing to understand more about the problems in Aletheia and how to help?" asked Henrietta.

Candour Communique considered for a moment. Then, "I think the Mustardseeds might benefit from a visit to the Prayer Academy," she said.

"Of course!" exclaimed Josie. "The Meddlers mentioned the *Power-Tower* the time I overheard them…[1]" She scribbled frantically on her pad.

Candour looked at Josie with renewed interest. "You're the girl that overheard the Blue-Stocking Meddlers," she said, realising now why the name 'Josie Faithful' had sounded familiar. For every Chief, Director, Head, and Manager in Aletheia had once heard the name 'Josie Faithful', in connection with the discovery of the plan of the Meddlers. "You played an important part in the discovery of the Meddlers' plan," said Candour.

Josie shrugged. "I think God allowed me to be there at the right time," she said. "And the Blue-Stocking Meddlers mentioned the Care-Caster," she added. "I remember now!"

Candour nodded. "Pay particular attention to the Care-Caster," she said.

Josie nodded earnestly, writing that down too. Candour watched her, thinking she would make a good reporter for *The Truth*. She was organised, and keen, and thorough. And she had a good memory for detail. It was thanks to her memory that the Meddlers' plans had been known at all.

Candour knew, because she had heard the story, that Josie Faithful had once rebelled against Aletheia and against God. She had been utterly, horribly broken and disgraced. But when she confessed her sin to God, He had made her completely whole again[1]. And now Josie was intent on working for the good of Aletheia: perhaps this might one day involve working for *The Truth*.

CHAPTER 9
THE SURVEY

Timmy and Hugo weren't having a particularly good afternoon. On the same day that Zek and Jack headed to the Judges' Academy, and Josie and Henrietta met with Miss Communique, Timmy and Hugo set off in fine form to 'scout out the city' and 'gather intelligence'. But the excitement of an afternoon off school, doing important research into the plan of the Meddlers, very quickly paled.

Firstly, Flair Scholar, having lost sight of Josie and Henrietta, and not thinking the two smaller boys were likely to be doing anything very interesting, plunged valiantly after Timmy and Hugo. The boys were not very far down steep, straight Pride Way when Flair hollered, "Hey! Hugo! Timmy! Wait up!"

Hugo, startled by this intrusion at the start of their mission, turned to see Flair stumbling down the steep road, her bulging satchel bouncing wildly around her body. "Oh, boy!" he muttered to Timmy. "This is all we need!"

"I thought you were going to go without me," panted Flair when she reached them. "You did say I could observe your meetings and...well, whatever else you're doing."

Hugo could not remember making such a wide-reaching promise, but, "We're only going to find out some of the opinions of the people on The Outskirts and gather information," he said.

"Great!" said Flair. "But it would be useful if you would tell me when and where you were going, so I know what's going on, you see?"

"Didn't you want to go with the girls?" asked Timmy.

Flair shrugged. "They didn't tell me where they were going either," she said. "I lost sight of them, and then I saw you!"

Hugo caught a fleeting glimpse of his younger brother Zek, and Jack, and...had Zek actually taken Hector to the Judges' Academy? Whatever were the boys up to? He couldn't remember exactly what tasks they had been given; no doubt they would all find out what each other had been up to at the next meeting of the Mustardseeds. But in the meantime he and Timmy needed something to show for their precious free afternoon.

"Where are we going first?" asked Flair cheerfully. She seemed immune to the strong impression both boys gave that she was not remotely wanted on this particular venture.

"To Law Villas," said Hugo.

"And what exactly are we going to do?" asked Flair eagerly.

"We're going to knock doors, and ask people the questions on our survey," said Hugo shortly. "But you promised not to interrupt, so you mustn't distract us."

"I promise," said Flair. "Could I just have a copy of your survey...?"

"No, you couldn't," said Hugo, becoming more exasperated by the minute.

"You'll hear us ask the questions," said Timmy.

"I'll help you record the answers," said Flair.

Neither Hugo nor Timmy had ever visited people in Law Villas before. From a distance they had both seen the smart, square, regimented block of villas that were all exactly the same. But they had never looked closely at the place, and never, to their knowledge, spoken to someone from this section of The Outskirts of Aletheia. The place was excessively neat and tidy, with bright, white walls, and black doors and window frames; every villa was precisely the same. But the most noticeable thing about Law Villas was the large number of small black and white signs that seemed to be rules and regulations. There were far too many to read, and, since they all looked the same, none stood out from any other.

Feeling hot in the unrelenting sun, and not a little fed up with Flair who was ready to record everything he said, Hugo knocked boldly on the first gleaming black door. It was opened almost immediately by a lady wearing a spotless white apron and carrying a basket of washing.

"That was *four short* knocks," she said anxiously. "Did you really

mean to knock *four* times, only *short* knocks?" She glanced furtively into the bright outdoors, where there was nothing in sight to unduly alarm her, only Flair writing in a book.

"Uh, I didn't really count the knocks," said Hugo, startled at the inquisition about knocking.

The lady sighed heavily. "Didn't you read the rules about knocking?" she asked. "You gave me quite a fright with *four* knocks!"

"No, ma'am," said Hugo politely, "sorry, ma'am."

"How many times should we knock?" asked Timmy, thinking of all the other doors they had yet to visit in this place.

The lady placed her basket of washing on the table in the hallway and looked at them with her hands on her hips. "You really haven't read our rules, have you?" she said.

"No, ma'am," said Hugo.

"Well, it depends what you're calling for, doesn't it?" the lady said. "One knock for coming-straight-in, twice for callers, three times for..."

"Uh, I think I should have knocked twice," said Hugo hastily. "I'm sorry, ma'am."

"Never mind," said the lady. "Well, what can I do for you?"

"We're conducting a survey," began Hugo.

"Will it take long?" asked the lady anxiously. "I have to hang my washing out in the next hour, or I can't hang it out until Friday. They're the rules, you see?"

Hugo didn't *see* at all but he didn't bother to say so. He was quickly coming to the conclusion that the folk living at Law Villas were barking mad.

"It's very quick," said Timmy, "just five questions, about the problems in Aletheia with Meddlers and prayer and such."

"Problems?" asked the lady suspiciously. "Meddlers? Have the chiefs in Aletheia resorted to using schoolchildren to stir up trouble? Dear me..."

"No, it's not like that at all," Hugo said hastily. "We're doing our own survey..."

"Well, please do it quickly then," said the lady, glancing at the clock on the wall. "What do you need to know?"

"Have you seen a Meddler?" asked Hugo, which was the first question he and Timmy had agreed upon.

"Seen a Meddler!" exclaimed the woman indignantly. "What do you take me for? Do you think I'm one of these paranoid people that find Meddlers everywhere I turn? Meddlers are in the heads of the people up there." She gestured towards the main city buildings clustered at the top of the hill around the cross. "They're just trying to get us to move back to the constraints of city-centre life..."

"We'll take that as a 'no' to the question then," murmured Timmy.

"Uh, I think we probably already know the answer to this next question," said Hugo, glancing with concern at his question number two which was: 'Are you worried about the reports of Meddlers in the city of Aletheia?'

The indignation on the lady's face was more than adequate answer to this question. "I'm worried about hanging my washing out in time within the rules, not Meddlers!" she exclaimed. "Is this all a conspiracy by the managers of Aletheia? Sending schoolchildren to ask their questions and..."

"No, it's honestly not that, ma'am," said Timmy.

"Just three more questions," said Hugo rather despondently.

"I hope they're better than the last ones," said the lady, and Flair, who was relishing the whole encounter, was heard to smother a giggle.

Hugo looked in discouragement at his next question: 'Do you think prayer is affected by the Meddlers?' He could make a very educated guess at this lady's response to that question, so he decided to move to question four instead.

"Uh, how often, uh, do you pray?" Hugo asked.

"How often do I pray?" asked the lady, and surprisingly, she didn't seem quite as offended this time. "Well, our new five-point prayer guide, which is currently going through various Committees, will sort all that out, won't it?"

"Will it?" asked Timmy. "Do you mean that they...that your, uh, Committees will tell you how often you should pray?"

"Well, of course they will!" said the lady. "How else would we know?"

Timmy, stunned into silence, glanced at Hugo. Hugo shrugged helplessly. "There's just one more question," he said, moving on.

"Good!" said the lady. "If I don't get my washing hung out soon..."

"Do you pray more often, or less often, since the reports of Meddlers coming...uh, coming to Aletheia...?" He trailed off uncertainly, realising it was yet another question which made no sense to this lady, just as her answers made no sense to him and Timmy.

"Well," said the lady, moving to pick up her washing basket again and brushing past them out of the door. "Well, that depends how many times it's specified we should pray when the new five-point prayer guide is issued, doesn't it? But I tell you one thing. All this talk about the Meddlers has driven us *to* prayer, not *from* it! That's why we're producing our five-point prayer guide! So, there's much more *talk* about prayer than there has been for many years!"

"I wonder if that means people actually pray," muttered Timmy, as they followed the lady to the washing lines. "Or do they only *talk* about it?"

"What else will the...uh, the five-point prayer guide contain?" asked Hugo, keeping up with the lady who made her way to one of several dead-straight washing lines all next to each other and all exactly the same. It occurred to him that, in this desperate place of rules and regulations, they ought to find out as much as they could about exactly what the folk here were doing about prayer, even if it wasn't on their survey.

"The five-point prayer guide will tell us things like how often to pray," the lady said, carefully selecting a blue peg to hang up blue socks, "and where we should pray, whether we should sit or kneel or stand to pray, what we should wear to pray, and..."

"And exactly what to say when you pray?" ventured Timmy.

"However did you guess?" asked the lady. She observed the three children, looking hot in the blazing spring sunshine. "I would offer you lemonade," she said, evidently feeling sorry for them. "I think it's a crying shame they've got you kids out here asking questions for their survey…"

"It's really not like that!" exclaimed Hugo.

"I expect it's not the right day to make lemonade, is it?" said Timmy gravely and politely.

The lady looked at him in admiration. "You're a very smart boy," she said. "However did you guess?"

They nearly gave up on Law Villas after that. But Timmy thought they ought to pursue their survey, with a few adaptations in the way they asked the questions, just to make sure the rest of the folk here thought the same. The job was made decidedly easier by all of the ladies in Law Villas appearing in matching white aprons, with matching laundry baskets, all hanging out their washing on lines side by side, with colour-coded pegs for clothing items. Hugo did his part and then sat on the grass, defiantly choosing the spot close by the 'Keep off the grass' sign. Flair sat down beside him and chatted happily about the things she had learned about Law Villas. She, at least, was having a great time. Timmy valiantly continued to question the ladies hanging out their washing and nodded politely at their answers, scribbling on the notepad. Hugo watched his friend with amusement. At one point Timmy was very nearly entangled in a sheet waving in the breeze, with two eager ladies telling him all he wanted to know.

"He's quite the charmer, isn't he?" said Flair brightly, looking admiringly at Timmy.

"I'm sure he'll be pleased you think so," said Hugo drily.

"They've all lost the plot a bit here though, don't you think?" continued Flair.

"Yes, they have a bit," Hugo admitted.

"What's different out here?" asked Flair. "I mean, in the centre of Aletheia people never talk like that about prayer and stuff, do they?"

"I think it's because the people here have chosen to live on The Outskirts," said Hugo. "You know, away from the cross."

"Oh," said Flair. "Is the cross what makes the difference? Is that what makes people pray and take things seriously?"

Hugo had been taught the answer to that question for as long as he could remember. He knew the answer even before he had trusted in the Lord Jesus and became a Christian. But when he became a Christian he found it was true for himself. "Yes," he said. "The closer you are to the cross, the better Christian you are, including in prayer and stuff. It's about being close to the Lord Jesus, you see, and remembering everything He has done for you. Then you take the Christian life more seriously."

"That's useful, very useful," said Flair, and she scribbled this down on her pad which already contained plenty of information for the Importance of Sanctification and Prayer assignment.

Hugo watched Flair writing eagerly all he had said. Flair wasn't even a Christian. She was thinking about this whole thing – the plan of the Meddlers, the attack on Aletheia, the school assignment – purely as an academic exercise to get the highest marks and win the prize. For the first time, Hugo considered her as someone God might have sent to the Mustardseeds for a reason. Flair was someone who needed to be saved.

When Timmy finished questioning the ladies at the washing lines, they gave each of the children a drink of water: it was a 'water-only day' at Law Villas.

"If you'd come tomorrow, you would have got lemonade!" said a lady.

The three children began the steep ascent of Pride Way, back to the city at the top.

"Perhaps there's a five-point guide to what to drink too," Timmy muttered to Hugo.

"Did you taste that water?" exclaimed Hugo. "I didn't want to be rude, but that wasn't proper Water of Sound Doctrine!"

"It certainly wasn't!" agreed Timmy.

"I thought it was alright," said Flair.

Neither of the boys commented on the fact that Flair thought the water at Law Villas tasted alright. To them it confirmed their suspicions that the Water of Sound Doctrine that was piped to the houses in Law Villas had been adjusted to suit the taste of the people. All the Christian kids in Aletheia were well aware that if the pure Water of Sound Doctrine didn't taste right to a Christian, then there was something wrong with the person – not the water. And if you continually drank Water of Sound Doctrine which had been altered or polluted, then you began to lose sight of the Truth altogether – until you became like the people in Law Villas, relying on rules and regulations instead of the Truth contained in the Bible.

"Do you know one thing I asked the ladies which wasn't on our survey sheet?" said Timmy.

"Something clever or nice, I expect," guessed Flair. To Hugo's great, but hidden, amusement, Flair was walking close by Timmy's side, looking at him in a sickly-sweet admiring way. Timmy gave her a startled, not entirely pleased, glance and Hugo artfully stifled a laugh.

"What was it you asked?" he said.

"I asked what four short knocks meant," said Timmy.

Flair giggled. "Imagine thinking of that!" she said.

"You'll never guess," said Timmy, now directing his comments exclusively to Hugo.

"Go on," said Hugo, amused.

Timmy grinned. "Among other things, it seems that four short knocks means that hang-out-the-washing time is cancelled!" he said.

CHAPTER 10
IN MR STRAW'S BARN

It was Jack who solved the problem of finding a private, available, comfortable meeting place for the Mustardseeds. Once he had seen Mr Straw's barn, he was convinced it should be their headquarters. As Zek's tastes ran in a similar vein – farm smells, the comforting sounds of snuffling, well-fed animals, the soothing presence of small, mainly nocturnal creatures, a place where Hector felt at home – both boys made an appeal to the older Mustardseeds which was not denied. In any case, none of the others, busy with their own tasks, had had the time to find a meeting place. Jack and Zek spoke to Mr Straw, and the second meeting of the Mustardseeds was convened. Flair Scholar, who haunted their footsteps and refused to be left out of anything, came too.

Jack and Zek went early to Mr Straw's barn on the evening of the gathering of the Mustardseeds. They worked with him to arrange bales of straw and hay and a couple of crates around the barn. Mr Straw, secretly much amused at the Mustardseeds' idea of a venue, and wishing he could exchange the Management Meetings at the Academy of Soldiers-of-the-Cross for the Mustardseeds' meeting, provided a big jug of milk, some glasses, and a plate of chocolate biscuits. Zek and

Jack were extremely proud of their arrangements. Hector was equally delighted. He licked out two clean glasses, and then he licked the chocolate from the top of one of the biscuits.

"It's not as if Hector's got *germs!*" said Zek loyally.

"It could be a biscuit without chocolate on the top of it," said Jack, considering the biscuit from all angles before poking it beneath the others.

"And the glasses look as clean as they did," said Zek.

Jack agreed. Then they both kept guard at the door of the barn, neither of them observing Hector drinking from the milk jug while Fly, Mr Straw's dignified collie, watched in disgust.

The Mustardseeds assembled, and Jack and Zek were very gratified by the general approval of their meeting place.

"Just right!" said Timmy.

"Couldn't have done better," agreed Hugo.

"Smell the country air!" said Dusty with a grin.

"I was trying to avoid that," murmured Josie good-naturedly.

"It's great, Jack and Zek," said Henrietta. "Just great!"

"It's just a bit, you know..." Flair entered last, looking dismayed at the surroundings.

"Not really," said Dusty. "Can't imagine anything better at a meeting than the appearance of the odd mouse, or rat..." He was amused at the squeals of protest from Flair and Josie. "Wish I could introduce them to some of Mr Buffer's meetings!" added Dusty.

After that, Josie sat with her feet tucked up under her on a bale of hay, and Flair jumped nervously at every snuffle or noise.

"I don't mean to be a nuisance," said Flair as they handed out glasses of milk to everyone. "But do...do these *dogs* have to be here? I really *don't like* dogs!"

Fly, the collie, lay quietly in the corner, not dignifying that remark with any attention whatsoever. Hector, though, was different. He immediately made his way to Flair and licked her bare toes through her sandals.

Flair squealed in protest.

"Zek," said Hugo, "maybe you could keep Hector on your bale between you and Jack?"

Zek, most alarmed at the thought of what Hector might catch from licking Flair's toes, was more than happy to comply. He and Jack had taken a very comfortable second tier hay bale, which they had earlier carefully placed for themselves. They had a great view and looked down on the assembled Mustardseeds with great satisfaction. And when Flair took the only plain biscuit – because she didn't like chocolate – Zek nudged Jack, and Jack nudged Zek, and both boys grinned.

"Now, let's get on with the business of the meeting," said Hugo. "Jo, I believe we have…"

"An agenda," said Josie, who, efficient as ever, had arrived thoroughly prepared. She distributed neat, hand-written agendas to everyone. Even Flair had a copy. Hugo had spoken to them all privately about being kind to Flair: she needed to be saved and she ought to see in the Mustardseeds something of the Lord Jesus[11]. All of them agreed, although it hadn't occurred to Zek that he would have to be kind to her despite the fact that she didn't like Hector.

"The first thing on the agenda is, uh, apologies," said Hugo. "What exactly does '*apologies*' mean, Jo?"

"That's what you put on for people who aren't here," said Josie.

"I know about that…" began Flair.

"Well, we're all here," said Hugo decisively, "so that's the first item dealt with. Now, item two, update from Dusty – which is intelligence on the situation in Err and Aletheia from the Academy of Soldiers-of-the-Cross."

It all sounded rather grand; they were very glad they had Dusty with his inside knowledge of things that only adults usually knew about.

"Right," said Dusty cheerfully. He rummaged about his pockets, eventually extracting a couple of scrunched up, stained sheets of paper with some writing on them. "I took notes of all the latest readings on the relevant monitors in the Central Control Room," he said. "The Prayer Power Monitor..."

"You mean there are machines that record and monitor things like prayer?" asked Flair incredulously.

Hugo sighed. "Perhaps you could explain briefly what each machine does as we go through, Dusty?" he suggested. "That might help Jack too."

"And me," said Timmy. "I haven't seen the Control Room yet."

Flair smiled a very special smile at Timmy. "Me too, Timmy," she said.

Timmy didn't take any notice.

"What's got into her?" hissed Henrietta.

"Never mind," said Hugo, trying not to laugh at Flair's continuing admiration of Timmy. He cleared his throat. "Right, Dusty, on you go..."

Dusty munched his second chocolate biscuit as he talked. "The Prayer Power Monitor is an *awesome* machine!" he said. "It records incoming prayer, assigns specific prayer to the right place, shows who is praying, shows the prayer power available for individuals and towns and Regions in Err, and shows overall prayer power too."

"Wow!" Jack tried to imagine such a machine. He wondered if it also showed a list of people who didn't pray enough. How awful it would be to be featured as a low- or non-prayer!

"This has got to be a big part of the Importance of Prayer assignment!" muttered Flair as she scribbled frantically on her notepad.

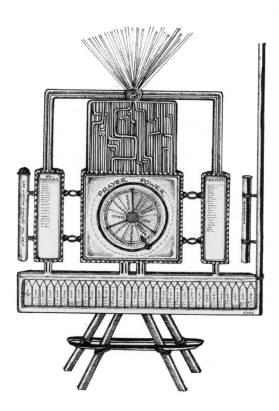

"I took an overall reading from the Prayer Power Monitor," said Dusty. "And I'm afraid it's not good."

It was as if every one of the Mustardseeds held their breath, such was the sudden stillness in the barn. Hector stopped biting the twine on the bale, and even Flair stopped her scribbling.

"There's a total of nine readings on the dial," said Dusty. "They range from number nine – which is green and shows *Strong* prayer power – which is really excellent and means that everyone is praying as they ought to be – to number one, the red *Danger* zone – which means that hardly anyone is praying and we could all fail at any moment!"

"Well?" prompted Hugo. "Is it...is prayer power falling so much?"

Dusty nodded soberly. "For the first time since I've been at the Academy the needle moved through category three and nearly into category two – which is *Imminent Danger*."

"Has it...has that happened much in the past?" asked Henrietta.

Dusty shook his head. "I asked Mr Buffer," he said. "He was pretty sick about the whole thing. He can't remember the last time we sank so low." Mr Buffer was the Central Control Room Manager. There was nothing Mr Buffer didn't know about the workings of the machines and devices in his Control Room.

"That's serious," said Hugo.

"I think we know that, Hugo," said Henrietta.

"We need an action point for this," said Josie, pen poised above her pad. "We need to pray!"

"Yes," agreed Timmy. "We need to carry on our investigations, of course, but we need to meet and pray too. Otherwise we're just like the people at Law Villas who only talk about prayer instead of praying!"

"Right," agreed Hugo. "Jo, note that the Mustardseeds will meet every morning before school..."

"Before school!" exclaimed Henrietta.

"It's the only time we have," said Hugo. "We'll use the empty classroom, which is still empty, and *pray!*"

They all nodded. Even Henrietta, not anxious to get up at the crack of dawn every day, agreed they must pray.

"Uh, can I come to this too?" asked Flair, raising her hand in the air.

"It doesn't seem to be easy to stop you," said Timmy.

Henrietta giggled and Flair, taking Timmy's comment as active encouragement, looked delighted.

Dusty continued with his report, taking them through fascinating readings from machines such as the Storm Tracker ("nothing on the horizon"); the Weather Guide ("unusually hot, dry, spring weather to continue for some time"); the Rascal Register ("off the radar on Meddlers and Fretters" – which didn't surprise anyone); the Aletheia Alert ("appears to be giving faulty, conflicting readings, which is worrying Mr Buffer"); the Water Sensor ("some strange readings which we can't work out, but no one has any time to spend on this just now"), and other devices and instruments besides.

"That's great, Dusty," said Hugo, when Dusty finished his report. "Really helpful. Anyone got any questions for Dusty before we move on?"

Josie looked at a list of neatly penned questions she had thought of in advance. "Uh, I've heard my brother say there are huge numbers of Rescuers away from Aletheia just now. It's surely more than coincidence that so many of our Rescuers are absent from Aletheia, just when they're needed at home. Could this be part of the Meddlers' plan?"

"Good thinking, Jo!" exclaimed Timmy.

Flair looked rather resentfully at Josie.

"Is it possible to get information about the numbers of Rescuers absent and why?" Hugo asked Dusty.

"It might take some digging," said Dusty. "But I'll have it ready for the next meeting!" That was one of the nice things about Dusty. He had no pretentions to leadership; he simply knew what he was meant to be doing, and did it with cheerfulness and enthusiasm.

"Right, now to item three on the agenda," said Hugo. "Update from Jo and Henry on their visit to Miss Communique at *The Truth* newspaper."

The girls had already shared much of the information they had gleaned with the other Mustardseeds. They all knew about the possible threat of a Green-Jacket Meddler attack, and the results this would have on the precious food supplies to the city of Aletheia.

"But there are a couple of things we need to follow up for Miss Communique," said Josie, consulting her notes. "Firstly, and this is important, Miss Communique needs to interview Mr Straw, who we know is the representative of Pray-Always Farmlands. She needs first-hand information about...uh..."

"About sightings of the Green-Jacket Meddlers, and any evidence of blight," completed Henrietta. "That would help them to assess the threat. We told Miss Communique we'd arrange it. Mr Straw will be OK with that, won't he, Zek?"

Zek shrugged. "I expect so," he said. He had no fear of interviews with unknown females; it didn't occur to him that shy Mr Straw might have. "I'll go and fetch him," announced Zek. And, climbing off his bale, with Hector tripping him up on the way down from his perch, he disappeared through the barn door into the spring twilight where the sun was sinking low in the sky.

"The other thing," continued Josie, "is that Miss Communique recommended a visit to the Prayer Academy."

"And particularly to the Care-Caster," added Henrietta.

"That's a good idea," said Hugo. "We could ask the Prayer Academy Director, Mr Stalwart, about that."

"Don't forget to let me know the arrangements," said Flair. "Timmy, you'll tell me, won't you?"

"You seem to find out everything anyway," said Timmy, clearly startled to be singled out in this way.

Flair appeared pleased with his response and Henrietta stifled her laughter.

"Now," said Hugo, consulting the handy agenda. "Oh! Mr Straw! Please come in, sir, we needed your, uh, opinion..."

Mr Straw entered the barn with great interest. It was nothing like the usual quiet, restful place that he sometimes resorted to at the end of a hardworking day, to enjoy the scents and sounds of his well-fed animals. Instead, eight children were perched around a small circle on his bales and crates, planning, as Zek had told him, the defence of Aletheia and the overthrow of the Meddlers.

"Honoured to attend," said Mr Straw, with a twinkle in his eye.

"Actually, we need a favour," said Henrietta.

"Go on," said Mr Straw.

"Are there any more chocolate biscuits?" asked Zek.

Mr Straw suddenly laughed.

"Zek!" exclaimed Henrietta. "That wasn't the favour we were going to ask Mr Straw!"

"Wasn't it?" said Mr Straw. "I hope the real one is as easy!"

"It's about Miss Communique," said Henrietta in her usual blunt style.

"Miss-Miss Communique?" faltered Mr Straw, his ruddy face turning a deeper hue.

"She wants to interview you."

"About the Green-Jacket Meddlers and the possibility of blight on the fruit and crops," explained Josie more helpfully. "We were interviewing her for our project, you see, and she thought it would be helpful if..."

"Well-well," said the clearly astonished Mr Straw, clearing his throat. "Young Zek here knows as much as I do about these things. He saw a Green-Jacket..."

"We can be interviewed together," said Zek, clambering back onto his bale, with Hector growling and yanking at his trousers. "Down, Hector!" said Zek. "You can't tear another pair of trousers!"

Mr Straw retreated to his farmhouse to consider the Mustardseeds and the sudden intrusion – both good and bad – into his comfortable, bachelor life. Then he filled another plate full of chocolate biscuits and, with the amused twinkle back in his eye, took them to the barn to restock the Mustardseeds. He was puzzled when the girl he didn't know asked for "another one of the plain biscuits"; but, when he observed Jack and Zek giggling, he was wise enough not to enquire.

Hugo and Timmy gave their report of their visit to Law Villas, peppered with a few comments from Flair. "And, if I may be allowed to mention one more thing," added Flair at the end of the report.

"Well?" said Hugo rather warily.

"In his school address, Mr Mustardpot mentioned learning about something called *Sanctification*, and it *is* part of the assignment. I just wondered what you're going to do about that?"

"I thought about that too!" said Zek. "But I forgot the word."

"I think Timmy and I will take that on," said Hugo. "Mr Mustardpot mentioned a building on the corner of Redemption Square which is called Sanctification. We'll visit there."

"Just let me know when you're going and I'll be there," said Flair, scribbling one last note in her book.

The meeting was nearly concluded. Hugo came to the last item on the agenda, which was 'Update from Zek and Jack'.

"Anything to add, boys?" he asked.

"Apart from more chocolate biscuits," said Henrietta, grinning at her younger brother.

"We're researching Meddlers and Fretters," said Jack.

"It's all in here," added Zek. And he picked up a scruffy folder, bound in bailer twine from Mr Straw's supplies, and indicated numerous bits of paper which contained unknown things. "Mr Straw says we must know our enemies."

"That's actually a really good idea!" said Dusty.

"But we're not quite ready to give our report," explained Zek. "We've got more work to do."

"Important work," said Jack.

Zek nodded solemnly. "Very important work," he said.

CHAPTER 11
MR MUSTARDPOT'S DISCOVERY

Mr Mustardpot walked slowly down the empty corridor in Goodness and Mercy High School. The children had all gone home for the day, and it was a habit of the Headmaster's to tour his schools, investigate random classrooms, glance at notice boards, check the registers and discipline books, and generally enjoy the unusual quiet in the school. It was usually a time of relief and reflection, but of late Mr Mustardpot was despondent. He was a man of decisive activity, and this slowly-waged war of tiny, puny imps called Meddlers, an enemy they could hardly see, did not suit his active personality. He was pleased that a small group of Rescuers, the few that could be spared, were out searching for the Meddler Pod which the managers knew must be active somewhere close to – or even within the boundaries of – Aletheia. He would like to personally deal with the Meddlers and their Pod-home if they were ever found. And he would definitely like to be out in the meadows, *pulverising* the Meddlers that were rumoured to be even now wiping horrid blight-goo on the precious budding fruit and crops.

And that was nothing to what he'd like to do to Team WondERRful, the representatives of Err who wanted to sign up to the international Revolting Nations Agreement. The managers of Aletheia were all well aware that signing the Revolting Nations Agreement would only strengthen ties with the awful land of Iniquitous. It would make the battle for the Truth, in which Aletheia was engaged, even harder; it would multiply their enemies; Aletheia would be up against the combined might of Err and Iniquitous; the city might even be defeated!

Just today, Team WondERRful had sent hundreds of leaflets to Mr Mustardpot's schools in Aletheia, targeting the young people, encouraging them to be ready to join Team WondERRful as the much-needed Aletheian – or *Region 15* as Err called it – representative. Mr Mustardpot could barely remember a time that the influence of Err had reached its tendrils so far into Aletheia. With good prayer cover these leaflets would never have got into his schools. And now they were recruiting children to represent Aletheia and ensure so-called Region 15 was represented in signing the Revolting Agreement! None of the managers had ever considered that Team WondERRful might target the *children* of the city and find a representative there!

It was with these gloomy forebodings that Mr Mustardpot opened the door of the empty classroom on the top floor corridor. The classroom had recently been decorated but didn't appear to be back in use. He must check with Joe, the Caretaker, about that in the morning. He was about to leave the room when he noticed that someone had left some written notes on a table. Intrigued, he lifted the first sheet and read 'Prayer Meeting of the Mustardseeds', which was followed by a list of items, each of which had been neatly marked with a tick.

"The Mustardseeds," murmured Mr Mustardpot, strangely cheered. "I wonder what made them think of that..."

He read through the prayer items one by one:

1. Against the Meddlers and Fretters (which was underlined twice)

2. For all Adults to Pray

3. The Outskirts people – to stop their silly issues

4. For Whiskers who looks so tired

5. To visit the Prayer Academy

6. For Hector & Fly to catch Meddlers and Fretters (this had 'Zek's & Jack's request' in brackets after it)

For the first time that weary, defeated day, Mr Mustardpot smiled. "Pray for Whiskers who looks so tired," he repeated with a smile. He had long known the nickname the children thought so secret. "Whiskers indeed!" And when he left the classroom he had the list in his pocket. "I'll return it later," he murmured, "but it might be of interest if we need cheering up at the Management Meeting!"

The birdsong of a spring twilight resounded around Aletheia when Mr Mustardpot walked across the city to the Management Meeting at the Academy of Soldiers-of-the-Cross. It was hard to imagine there was anything sinister at work against the grand, old city.

Mr Mustardpot made his way down familiar corridors, up winding staircases, on a quick ride down a moving passageway, and came at last to the Chief's own suite of rooms, deep in the fortress Academy. He no longer kept count of his visits here, or of the hours he spent with good and important people trying to plan the defence of Aletheia against an all-but-invisible foe. But one unexpected result that had arisen from these meetings was the new friends he had made. Friends he might never have met but for the strange circumstances that found them all joining forces for the sake of the city of the Truth. He saw one of these friends on entering the room and immediately made his way to the side of Mr Croft Straw.

"Good evening, Croft," said Mr Mustardpot.

"Oh, it's you, Philologus," said Croft Straw. Philologus Mustardpot didn't intimidate Croft Straw; somewhat unexpectedly they had become the oddest friends and comrades.

"You look anxious, man," said Mr Mustardpot robustly. "Just the usual meeting jitters, eh?"

"Something like that," muttered Croft.

"I'll join you if I may, gentlemen," said another man, as their other friend, an odd third to the strange trio of friends, joined the huddle at the end of the table. This man was Dr Theo Pentone, Director of Health in Aletheia. He was widely regarded as the cleverest man in the city, although he generally didn't look like anything of the sort. He had a rather distinguished-looking goatee-beard, but he wore everything but his long, white lab coat very badly. The suits he wore to the frequent Management Meetings were always crushed or stained with dubious-looking liquids. Croft Straw, in all his discomfort in his pressed tweeds and now familiar cow tie, looked smarter than Dr Pentone did in his scruffy suit and askew tie.

"Something up, Croft?" queried Dr Pentone.

"There is an important matter I must report to the meeting," said Croft. "There's been a sighting of a Green-Jacket Meddler in the apple blossom."

Of course, there had been plenty of rumours of sightings of Green-Jacket Meddlers. But it was the fact that Croft Straw was worried that bothered his friends. Croft knew all there was to know about the Green-Jackets of blight and their effect on farming.

"You think this is serious?" asked Dr Pentone.

Croft nodded. "It was a sighting by a reliable source," he said, choosing not to describe Zek Wallop to these clever men, who might not be so inclined to view him as reliable. "But there's more than that. I've kept an eye on the apple tree where the Green-Jacket was sighted..."

"Go on," said Philologus, but there was dread in his tone.

"Only this morning I found the blossom is blighted; withered and gone; even with Restorative I don't think there's a single apple that could be saved from that tree!"

Theo Pentone drew a sharp breath.

"And you haven't heard my news yet!" exclaimed Philologus. "Is there no end to these creatures' ability to meddle?"

"We'll draw the meeting to order and begin," said the Chief from the end of the long table.

"But you'll have to tell them about the Green-Jacket Meddler, old man," whispered Theo to Croft Straw. "This is too vital to miss!"

CHAPTER 12
THE MANAGEMENT MEETING

It was a pretty depressing Management Meeting. There was plenty of information, speculation, and predictions; there were numerous sightings of Meddlers, discussion about lack of resources, and the ever pressing problem of lack of prayer power. Mr Mustardpot, forthright and blunt, updated the meeting regarding the now widely publicised Revolting Nations Agreement, and the targeting of schoolchildren to represent Aletheia and ensure the signing of the Agreement would succeed. A few of the most senior managers at the meeting, including the Chief, were already suspicious that Err would think of a way around the refusal of Aletheia to enter the Agreement. But as prayer power weakened, so did their ability to keep this error from the city and from the schools. Mr Mustardpot's assignment about Sanctification and Prayer was losing in the battle for the students' attention. All of the managers knew that the Truth of Sanctification would keep at least the Christian children safe from interest in the Agreement in Err. But not many had yet explored what this meant, and even the prize of one hundred house points was nothing to the allure of Iniquitous and the gifts of Err.

"The Council of Err – or Team WondERRful, as they're calling their representatives – know they need to have every Region in Err represented in order to sign up to the Agreement," said the Chief.

"But we don't even consider ourselves an official *Region* of Err," said Mr Hardy Wallop, the Superintendent of Entry into Aletheia. "I know the Council of Err act as if we're Region 15 and in collusion with them, but we've always acted independently. How could we do otherwise when we can't possibly agree with Err?! We hold the Truth, and that, as we all know, is utterly opposed to the aims of the land of Err!"

"Agreed," said the Chief firmly. "But I think there is a deeper, darker agenda at work here. I received a letter from Governor Genie, the Head of the Council of Err. She appeals to our sense of community, reason, justice, and plenty of other things besides." Mr Mustardpot snorted in disgust, and the Chief continued. "The most obvious answer is for the land of Err to simply remove us as a Region, or pretend we're part of another Region, or some such other solution. But they won't do it."

"Why not?" asked Roger Stalwart, Director of the Prayer Academy.

"Because they want Aletheia to be part of Err. They want us compromised, or amalgamated, and eventually, I don't doubt, they want us completely overcome and changed into the mould of Err."

"That's always been their aim," agreed the Chief Judge, Sagacia Steady.

"And I think that is what's behind the plan of the Meddlers, and behind this Revolting Agreement too," said the Chief. "And if we won't give them what they want – and that's an official representative to join Team WondERRful which they need in order to sign the Revolting Nations Agreement – then they will change the rules and ensure they get it anyway!"

"Which is exactly what's happening with this lowering of the age limit for the representative for Aletheia!" growled Mr Mustardpot.

"Precisely, Philologus," agreed the Chief.

"Can they lower the age limit and still enter?" someone asked.

"They do precisely what they want!" growled Philologus Mustardpot.

"You're right, Philologus," said the Chief. "They will do whatever it takes to try and see us compromised and engaged with them in their error and lies."

"They'll make a clever argument that they're being extra *rebellious* and *revolting* against rules and regulations by allowing a child to represent Aletheia," suggested the Chief Judge. "It will only make them seem liberal and enlightened to the organisers from Iniquitous."

"I guess this is the Meddlers' 'Distractions for the Young' plan being fully revealed at last," observed Candour Communique.

The Chief nodded slowly. "I hadn't seen the link so clearly until now, Candour," he said.

"Is this where we should be focussing our prayer power?" asked Roger Stalwart of the Prayer Academy. "Against the efforts of Team WondERRful to recruit a student to represent Aletheia?"

"I believe so," said the Chief. "This appears to be the most imminent danger."

The stumbling account of Mr Croft Straw, given after the colourful account of Mr Mustardpot, failed to impress the managers as the priority situation on which prayer should be focussed. Mr Mustardpot felt very sorry for his friend, Croft; he knew how seriously he took the potential blight of the Meddlers.

"If I could crave your indulgence, Chief," Mr Mustardpot said when business had almost drawn to a close. "I have a further matter to mention."

"Of course, Headmaster," said the Chief.

Mr Mustardpot withdrew the Mustardseeds' Prayer Meeting plan from his pocket and held it up before the Chiefs, Heads, Directors, Managers, and every senior Rescuer in Aletheia. He described finding it in an empty classroom; he read off the items for prayer that the children had penned, causing amusement with the item about 'Whiskers'. "They call themselves the Mustardseeds," he said, "and I think we all know why. And if these children truly have faith the size of a mustard seed..."

"Nothing is impossible,[7]" completed the Chief.

"I just thought it would encourage us all!" said Mr Mustardpot, glancing especially at his friend Croft Straw. "We're up against it, no doubt about that, but our God can still do impossible things[12] if we have the faith to ask! And these terrible Meddlers that we can't defeat because we don't have the prayer power and can't even find their wicked Pod-home – well, that's nothing to our God!"

There were smiles and even the odd tear across the room of weary, anxious faces.

"Did you say the Mustardseeds?" asked the Chief Judge with interest.

"I've met a couple of the Mustardseeds," said Miss Communique. "I was interviewed by them. It seems, Philologus, that they're not so much interested in your prize assignment about prayer, as in saving Aletheia and defeating the Meddlers!"

"God bless them!" said the astonished Headmaster.

"I understand that Croft is initiated into their, uh, secrets," said Miss Communique, with a glint of teasing she couldn't resist. Mr Straw went red in the face.

"Are you really, Croft?" asked Mr Mustardpot.

"They meet in my barn," admitted Croft. "But I think they consider themselves a, uh, secret organisation..."

"A secret organisation?" chimed in the Chief Judge, Miss Steady.

"Well, strange to say, I had an encounter with two of the Mustardseeds at the Judges' Academy. They were researching Meddlers and Fretters!"

"They've been praying to visit the Prayer Academy, you say?" said Roger Stalwart, the Director of the Prayer Academy. "Well, we shall just have to make sure it happens, then!"

At the end of the meeting Philologus Mustardpot and Theo Pentone were most amused to watch their friend Croft Straw go cap in hand to the dazzling, teasing Miss Candour Communique.

"No wonder poor Croft was so anxious tonight!" Philologus whispered to Theo. "The Mustardseeds have somehow convinced him to be interviewed by Candour Communique!"

CHAPTER 13
INTERVIEW WITH MISS COMMUNIQUE

Three interesting, perhaps surprising, things happened after the Management Meeting. Hugo and Timmy, who had carefully prepared a very polite request to see Mr Roger Stalwart of the Prayer Academy regarding a tour of his most impressive establishment, received a puzzling response from the front door guard at the Prayer Academy.

"I'm afraid Mr Stalwart is extremely busy these days," said the man. "You might have to wait a week or two – oh, but wait a minute..." The man in the smart uniform of the Prayer Academy consulted a book at his desk by the front door. "Are you, by any chance, the children known as the Mustardseeds?" he asked.

Considerably surprised, Hugo stuttered, "Yes-yes, sir."

"Then I'm instructed to give you all an entry pass for the Prayer Academy," said the guard. "How many would that be for?"

"There are seven of us..." began Timmy.

"Eight – there's Flair," said Hugo.

"Uh, eight...what about Hector?" added Timmy, who was very partial to Hector himself.

"I'm not sure..." Hugo began uncertainly.

"*All* the Mustardseeds are welcome," said the guard. "They're my instructions. I'll make that nine passes, shall I?"

"Thank you!" said Timmy, collecting nine smart gold pins from the guard.

"Come whenever it suits you," said the man cheerfully.

"Uh, right," said Hugo. "Thank you very much, sir!"

"Just doing my job," said the man. "You Mustardseeds must be quite important for the boss to give away so many entry passes in these difficult, dangerous times!"

The two boys hurried away before he could change his mind. "How on earth...?" began Hugo.

"How did he know about the Mustardseeds? I have no idea!" said Timmy. "It can only be..."

"An answer to our prayer list!" said Hugo.

It was the only possible explanation.

The second interesting thing that resulted from the Management Meeting was that the Important People, who were the busiest people in Aletheia, began, in ones and twos, to meet with their friends to pray. They had already been praying, of course, but they had been strangely touched by the revelation that a group of schoolchildren were getting up early in the morning to meet in a deserted classroom to pray for the defeat of the Meddlers and the safety of Aletheia. And so, Miss Candour Communique, who was already up at the crack of dawn, got up earlier still and met with two old school friends in one of their homes, and they drew up their own prayer list and prayed together. And Mr Hardy Wallop, Superintendent of Entry to Aletheia, met with his friend and brother-in-law Mr Sturdy Wright who was the Head Keeper of the Water of Sound Doctrine, and they prayed together in the early hours of the morning before their frantically busy days began. And Dr Theo Pentone trudged across the dew-drenched pasture of Pray-Always Farmlands and started the day in prayer with Mr Croft Straw, just before two boys and one small dog ran across the fields to see their farmer friend.

The third interesting thing that happened following the Management Meeting was that Miss Candour Communique was going, at last, to interview Mr Croft Straw. She set off for Croft Straw's interesting house early in the morning. Mr Straw had been quite specific about the timing of the interview. He had 'friends' he wanted to be present, one of whom was witness to the Green-Jacket Meddler discovered in the apple blossom tree. The tree had undoubtedly suffered awful blight; it had since lost the glory of its precious white flowers and the possibility of all its fruit too. It was exactly the type of evidence that Candour was looking for; the tree would show beyond doubt that at least part of the Meddlers' plan was to attack the food supplies of Aletheia.

Candour Communique might have been very smart and business-like in appearance, but she had taken the precaution of wearing stout, waterproof shoes for this particular venture. She thoroughly enjoyed her meander across Mr Straw's well-kept farmland, and the sight of his unique home too. There was the aroma of fresh coffee in the air as she knocked on the farmhouse door. Then there was the excited yap of a dog, followed by the opening of the front door, and the release of a small, white, scruffy bundle that briefly flung himself upon her, then raced away in joyful abandon, pursued in great indignation by a large collie. Miss Communique dropped her folder in the whirlwind of dogs and noticed she had the outline of a doggy print on her smart suit. But the inconvenience of that was forgotten in the first impressions she gained of Mr Straw's kitchen.

"Please take a seat," said Mr Straw, ushering her to a chair at the cluttered table.

There were two boys already present at the table. They had a scruffy folder and miscellaneous paperwork and pens and pencils strewn across the surface between them.

"Zek, I think Hector has greeted Miss Communique rather too enthusiastically," Mr Straw said to one of the boys

Candour realised that Croft Straw had definitely noticed the unfortunate paw print on her smart suit. He was barely hiding his amusement.

"Never mind," she said briskly.

"He does *like* people," said the boy called Zek, as if the paw print was a mark of the highest favour.

"Quite a lot, actually," added the other. "Fly does too."

"So I gather," said Candour, assuming that 'Fly' was the large collie that had chased the errant small dog from the farmhouse. "And are you the boys that spotted the Green-Jacket Meddler?"

"That's me," said Zek.

"I'm Jack," said Jack.

"Very nice to meet you," said Candour. It was intriguing to her to meet these younger members of 'the Mustardseeds', who had somehow succeeded in arranging this interview. "You have a very comfortable home, Croft," she added.

"Thank you," returned Mr Straw, as if he knew that perfectly well.

"Was that Dr Theo Pentone I saw leaving?" asked Candour.

Mr Straw nodded. "He's a friend," he said.

Candour had noticed the group of three close, very different friends – Croft Straw, Theo Pentone, and Philologus Mustardpot – that had grown out of their Management Meetings. She would like to have heard some of their conversations, but she was never invited to join them.

Mr Straw put a sturdy mug, full of coffee, in front of Candour and placed a plate of biscuits on the table.

"Sometimes Hector likes to lick out the coffee cups," Zek confided.

"Once he licked the chocolate off a biscuit!" said Jack.

"But, uh, not this morning..." began Mr Straw.

"Were these biscuits always without chocolate?" asked Candour, with a twinkle of amusement.

"Those are OK," said Zek. "Mr Straw made them himself."

"Why, Croft!" said Candour. "I never took you for a baker!"

Mr Straw went a dull red and cleared his throat. "Perhaps we should talk about the Meddlers?" he said.

"Right," said Candour briskly, and she removed her pad and pen.

The account of the sighting of the Green-Jacket was soon over, and they all visited the sad apple tree that was drooping with blight more and more each day.

Candour asked intelligent questions about the other crops and plants and vegetables and even animals that Mr Straw suspected might be prone to blight spread by the Green-Jacket Meddlers. What signs had he seen of them at work? Where? How bad did he think the problem could be?

"As bad as it's possible to be," said Mr Straw soberly.

"Suppose we have even lower prayer power, could individual Green-Jacket Meddlers really spread blight amongst our entire harvest?" asked Candour, as they all walked through the Pray-Always Farmlands fields on yet another glorious spring day.

"I don't think that's possible," admitted Mr Straw, "but I have my worries that..."

"Yes?" prompted Candour.

"Well, it's only what I think," said Mr Straw, "nothing I can prove. I just fear that, as well as the Meddlers training the Fretters to harass our old folk and stop them praying, the Meddlers have also trained Fretters to...well, to spread blight."

"But that would mean..." Candour trailed off in horror, the significance of this sinking in. And it seemed to the two boys listening to the conversation that the sun had slipped behind a big black cloud and the world had gone dark and shivery. It did nothing of the sort, but it was the sober dread in Mr Straw's next words that made them feel like that.

"Yes, that would mean *all* our food supplies would be lost," said Mr Straw.

CHAPTER 14
THE SEARCH FOR MEDDLERS

It was not in the nature of Jack or Zek to be satisfied with purely academic research. They were boys who enjoyed action, and when Mr Straw inadvertently planted the seeds of an active mission in their heads, they were not slow to formulate a plan. They understood very well their friend's real concern that the Meddlers had the capacity, through the pesky little Fretters that they trained and generally controlled, to destroy the entire food supplies of Aletheia. If Aletheians became reliant on food grown in Err and watered by the River Mee and the River Self, and other polluted and damaging waters in Err, then they would become weak Christians and would no longer hold the whole Truth of the Bible. And then Aletheia could fall altogether.

"We need to find the Meddler Pod," said Jack. They knew, through their painstaking research into the habits, homes, and other details of Meddlers, that Meddlers set up 'Pods' which were their temporary homes. They were usually located close to where they were at work, and Jack and Zek had heard the adults say that prayer cover was so low that meddlesome evil could have crept over the protecting Water of Sound Doctrine and settled where people lived out of sight of the cross. That meant that the Meddler Pod might be somewhere in The Outskirts of Aletheia!

They also knew from a previous adventure, when Josie had overheard the Blue-Stocking Meddlers' conversation inside the trunk of a tree[1], that it was possible, at least in theory, to discover and penetrate the secrets of the Meddlers. If only they could find that Meddler Pod and help Mr Straw discover if the Meddlers were going to use the Fretters to destroy all the crops.

The two boys prepared carefully – and secretly – for their mission to find the Meddler Pod, expecting God to answer their prayers to somehow secure a Meddler. They carefully designed a Meddler trap-cum-carrier, following the design suggested in an ancient book from the Judges' Academy which was long since out of print, and liberally borrowed material from Mr Straw to put the rather strange invention together. Hector, although integral to the plans, didn't appear to take the Meddler trap very seriously: he chewed a hole in it before it was even complete. Zek patiently mended the hole while Fly, Mr Straw's collie, looked on in disdain at Hector's undiminished glee. The older Mustardseeds, not initiated into the mysterious activities of the smaller boys, largely let them alone. They were, in any case, busy with their own tasks.

Zek had also 'borrowed' a map from his father's study. The map showed all The Outskirts of Aletheia – which was all the land and developments that were furthest away from the cross, but still within the boundary of the ever-flowing Water of Sound Doctrine. They pored over the map late at night, trying to determine where the most likely spot for a Meddler Pod might be. But it was no clearer the next time they examined it, than the time before. There was nothing on the map that indicated any clue to what they were seeking, and, more discouragingly, Mr Wallop had been heard to mention that Rescuers had already searched *all* of Aletheia for signs of the Meddler Pod and found nothing at all.

However, not to be put off their mission, the boys set off one free afternoon for Mr Straw's farm. They dressed in full armour of God[13], smeared dabs of camouflage on their cheeks, carried a rucksack and a stick each, and had various odd inventions and handy items around their persons. At Mr Straw's farm, they put into place the first part of their fairly sketchy plan – letting both dogs, Fly and Hector, sniff the blight-damaged blossom tree where Zek had spied the Green-Jacket Meddler. Hector barked loudly in response to Zek's command and ran rings around the tree, ending by getting confused and chasing his own tail. Fly watched the boys intelligently with her ears pricked up. She sniffed delicately where Jack indicated and wagged her tail.

"She's got it!" Jack said, "I think she knows the scent!"

They set off optimistically across the drenched fields on a day that was misty and damp and not spring-like at all. Fly headed south, followed closely by Hector who was still barking joyfully at whatever game he thought was intended. The dogs stopped a couple of times, which wasn't encouraging: neither of them appeared to be following any scent, but merely startled rabbits and birds and generally frolicked as if Meddlers weren't important at all. Jack and Zek encouraged them by shouts and the occasional throwing of a ball (one of the pieces of 'equipment' they had had the foresight to bring) and on they went, at a fairly smart pace, to The Outskirts of Aletheia.

They were approaching the very boundary of Aletheia – the deep, fast-flowing Water of Sound Doctrine – without the smallest, slightest evidence of Meddlers. Jack and Zek, ever optimistic, shouted encouragement to the dogs. Unfortunately the two dogs, not appreciating the dignity and importance of the expedition, at last made helter-skelter for the very thick, tangled vegetation surrounding No-Witness Apartments. And then they vanished altogether.

The prickly hedges and trees and shrubs and bushes planted around No-Witness Apartments were extremely dense, and the two boys pushed their way some distance into the bushes without catching a glimpse of the dogs. They followed Hector's constant excited yap, but then something happened.

Something strange and very unexpected.

Through the tangled greenery and trees and thorn bushes appeared a very weird, glittering pair of eyes. "Jack!" Zek said tremulously, unable to move. "Jack!"

Jack pushed through the scratchy bushes to join his friend. He kept his hand on his Bible. They were surely safe in Aletheia, and yet these were unpredictable days. Was it possible that they had found the lair of the enemy already...? Right outside of No-Witness Apartments? Jack, too, stopped and stared.

And stared.

And stared.

CHAPTER 15
DIM VIEW

The boys remained in their prickly prison, glued to the ground, scarcely daring to breath. They were hedged in by thick bushes and tall trees; they couldn't see the city of Aletheia at all. Was it possible that in this secluded place, next to the high walls of No-Witness Apartments, they were face to face with their enemies? They didn't know what to say but, oddly enough, it was the other thing, the thing-with-the-weird-eyes, that spoke first. "Are-are-are you Meddlers?" it stuttered in fright.

Jack and Zek were too astonished to speak. It was perhaps only the continual yapping of Hector, who did not like the thing-with-the-weird-eyes, that brought them to their senses.

"Who-who are you?" Jack managed to ask at last.

"Who-who-who are *you*?" returned the apparition.

"I'm Jack," said Jack, growing bolder.

"I'm Zek," said Zek, doing likewise.

"I'm Dim View," said the creature in the thicket.

"What, uh, what exactly is that?" asked Jack.

"I thought you were Meddlers," said Dim View, sounding braver and incredibly relieved.

"I don't know what we thought you were," said Zek frankly.

"We're Christians, not Meddlers!" said Jack.

The apparition slowly moved and extracted itself from the thicket where it appeared to have been moulded into a tree. Now that they could see it, they realised Dim View was actually a man – albeit an extremely odd old man. He was dressed in camouflaged clothing, with grass and twigs sticking out of his hair, and stripes of mud and berry juice on his wizened cheeks. In addition, he wore what looked like enormous swimming goggles which made his eyes seem strange and distorted and extremely weird when they were the only bit of him you could see. He really looked very peculiar indeed.

"You can't be too careful these days!" the old man said, as he pushed through the hedge to join the boys. He eyed Hector warily. Hector eyed him warily too and growled deep in his throat. Fly's ears were pinned back on her head. She looked very likely to nip Dim View and Jack kept his hand on her collar.

"Where do you live?" asked Zek, who was not usually given to caution, even with weird strangers.

"Here on The Outskirts, at No-Witness Apartments, of course," said Dim View.

"How do you get in?" asked Zek curiously. He couldn't imagine there was a way in through the tangled hedge and he had never seen a door into No-Witness Apartments. It seemed such an unwelcoming place. He had heard the adults say that the people who lived there liked to think that no one knew they were there. Quite why that was, Zek could not imagine.

"There's a secret door," said Dim View.

"Why?" asked Jack. "Don't you want visitors?"

Dim View looked confused at the question. "It's a wicked world," he said solemnly.

"That's why people need the Lord Jesus," said Zek matter-of-factly.

"What were you watching for?" asked Jack.

"Evil, wickedness, enemies!" said Dim. "It was my turn to stand guard, you see."

"In Aletheia?" asked Zek, frankly astonished. "Why don't you live close to the cross? You'd be safe then."

"End times are dangerous everywhere," said Dim View darkly.

Jack and Zek didn't understand that. Jack wondered why Mr View didn't wear his armour of God instead of the very strange disguise he had adopted. If he was fearful of a Christian's enemies, surely the armour of God would be far more helpful than sticks and twigs and swimming goggles!

"Did you happen to see any Meddlers when you were watching?" asked Zek hopefully.

"There is evil and iniquity on every side," said Dim. "We live in bad times. The day of nothings! The end is coming nigh!"

"That's why we're searching for Meddlers," said Jack, working his way through the muddle of Mr View's remarks to make some sense of them.

"Is it?" asked Zek, unable to make any sense at all of old Mr View and his opinions.

"Meddlers might attack Aletheia," said Jack. "We're looking for their Pod-home."

Mr View nodded slowly and mysteriously. Jack noticed the scratches on his face and hands from the thorn bushes. He felt sorry for the old man who was hiding in most unpleasant thickets, watching for enemies.

"There are voices," said Dim View in a hushed, confidential tone. "*Voices*! We know what's out there! Evil, iniquity! We must flee from it all!"

"But are there *Meddlers* out there?" asked Zek.

"*Voices*," repeated Dim. "You tell those folk at Aletheia about the *voices*!"

"Why don't *you* tell them?" asked Zek, somewhat exasperated by the mystery which Dim enjoyed when all Zek wanted was the plain truth.

Jack looked very doubtfully into the eyes of the mud-smeared face. Dim had two twigs of fresh green leaves sticking out from behind his ears. He didn't appear to be remotely in his right mind. "Where are, uh, the voices?" he asked.

"They sing," said Dim.

"Who do?" asked Zek.

"The *voices!*"

In none of their painstaking research into the types, habits, homes, and history of the Meddlers had Jack or Zek ever heard of Meddlers *singing*. They already knew that Meddlers liked silly rhymes: Jack had even heard them chanting one on a previous adventure[1]. But *singing...?*

"Uh, right," said Jack, disappointed that Dim View was proving so unreliably mad.

"They sing songs about Aletheia!"

The boys paused.

"*Where* do they sing?" prompted Jack cautiously.

Rather doubtfully, the boys and dogs followed the decidedly odd man, Dim View, further into the tangled mass of overgrown vegetation surrounding No-Witness Apartments. It was very deep and thick and there was barely a discernible opening at all. But Dim View pushed unerringly through the thorns and branches and, at last, stopped by a massive prickly gorse bush. He hushed them urgently to silence and Zek held Hector's mouth firmly shut, while Jack kept hold of Fly. Then they listened.

There was the singing of a bird somewhere close by. And they could hear the quiet, comforting murmur of the never ceasing Water of Sound Doctrine.

There was nothing else.

But then, very faintly, there was, in a Meddler-like childish voice, the words, "Beegan agin…"

And, to the boys' utter astonishment, the worst singing they had ever heard came faintly from somewhere in the interior of the gorse bush. There was no harmony; actually, no tune. None of the Meddlers could sing a note! But there was a weird wailing which reminded Jack of the bagpipes. And through the wailing a distinct rhythm, and the following words:

> "Thay squabble and thay do knott prayie
>
> The poison-blight will came [will came!]
>
> The Meddlers' plen is hear to stayie
>
> Alethie will succumbe [succumbe! succumbe! succumbe!]
>
> And now our cunningly thay will noo
>
> The cety walls will fell [will fell!]

Alethie is brought lew, so lew!

Know drinkie-drink at all! [at all! know drinkie-drink at all!]

It was the worst singing and the most stupid song the boys had ever heard. Zek, in his surprise at the Meddlers' singing, completely forgot about the dogs, and suddenly there were loud, penetrating barks from Hector who had escaped and was leaping in indignation at a creature buzzing around his head.

"Fretter!" cried Dim. "Woe is me! The Meddlers are upon us!" He made a sudden movement to flee and yelped in fright as Fly nipped him sharply on his ankle.

"Fly!" scolded Jack.

But there was no time to delay. Jack remembered very well what a Meddler attack was like and the buzzing Fretter had already vanished within the gorse thicket. If the Fretter was capable of warning the Meddlers that their silly song was being overheard, they didn't want a full-scale Meddler attack on them.

"Run, Zek!" Jack urged his friend. "Run!"

Dim View moved with incredible speed for such an old man. He forgot all about Fly's nip on his ankle and fled helter-skelter through the trees and shrubs and brambles, leaves and twigs falling into and out of his hair at every stride. He vanished entirely from view, leaving the two boys to struggle on through the tangled trees and bushes until at last, rather by chance, they stumbled through the last tangled branches and reached the open fields of Pray-Always Farmlands. The two dogs barked joyfully, and the two boys, torn, stained, looking almost as odd as Dim View, breathed a sigh of relief.

"I thought we might be onto something," said Zek regretfully, as they began to walk slowly up the sloping fields to Mr Straw's farm once more. "I thought we might hear something from the Meddlers about their plans. I thought that God would answer our prayers and that we might even catch a Meddler!"

Jack nodded. He had thought so too. They had prepared, they had prayed, so why hadn't God answered their prayers? They could never penetrate the gorse bush and grab one Meddler unawares. And besides, it had merely turned out to be a very silly *choir practice* – and how could they ever convince anyone of that? They doubted anyone would believe they had discovered a group of Meddlers *singing*.

In the end they decided to remain silent on the subject of their mission to find the Meddler Pod. "It's not as if we've got actual proof!" said Zek. "No one will believe us until we actually catch a Meddler or something!"

Jack agreed, accepting the reality that, unless they had some really good proof, none of the older Mustardseeds, and none of the grown-ups, were ever going to believe them. "Well, we'll just have to concentrate on Fretters instead," he said.

CHAPTER 16
THE PRAYER ACADEMY

Mr Mustardpot was being very generous with time off for the Importance of Sanctification and Prayer assignment. One afternoon, all of the Mustardseeds, including Flair and Hector, set off to visit the Prayer Academy with their nine gold-pin entry passes safely in Timmy's pocket.

"I thought old Whiskers might have been on to us this morning," admitted Hugo, as they walked across the city. It was odd, but when they had finished their early prayer meeting that morning, they spied the Headmaster loitering on the upstairs corridor, watching them leave the still unused classroom. Joe, the Caretaker, had never been instructed to put that classroom back into use. Mr Mustardpot considered it was being very well used already. He watched the children leave. There were a couple of surprises among them: Flair Scholar, who he knew wasn't a Christian, and a small, white dog called Hector.

"I'm sorry, sir," said Hugo Wallop politely to the Headmaster. "We thought that since the room wasn't in use…"

"That's alright, Wallop," said the Headmaster. "Carry on, carry on!"

Hugo was extremely surprised that the Headmaster's usually all-seeing eyes hadn't spotted the small dog Zek was trying to stuff under his jumper. Small, excited yaps from Hector, who thought it was a great game, had definitely been audible up and down the corridor – yet Mr Mustardpot had walked off as if he had not even heard them! Maybe Zek was right. Perhaps everyone *did* love Hector!

The Mustardseeds approached the vast, towering building which was the Prayer Academy.

"The power-tower," murmured Josie, remembering what she had overheard of the Meddlers' discussion – when they had spoken about the Prayer Academy as the 'power-tower'[1]. It was actually quite a good description. The tallest tower of the already tall Prayer Academy pointed far into the sky, the highest tower in Aletheia, taller than everything but the cross.

The Mustardseeds presented their gold-pin passes to the surprised front door guard. He wasn't the same guard who had given Hugo and Timmy the gold pins, and he looked somewhat askance at Hector's entry. But he didn't protest; unlikely though it seemed, Hector, too, had been granted a gold-pin pass.

The entrance hall was massive, swallowing up the space around it, echoing with unheard noises, still and calm, and mysterious in its quality.

"Almost as if someone is praying," whispered Henrietta.

They all walked purposefully towards the large, round, hollow pillar in the centre of the hall, as if they knew what they were doing. Which they did – sort of. They had informed Mr Wallop of their plans for the afternoon, and, since he had been present at the Management Meeting when the Mustardseeds' prayer list had been unveiled, it had not been difficult for him to discover the identity of the Mustardseeds. He had said nothing of that, however, just answered Hugo's enquiries regarding finding their way around the Prayer Academy.

"Go to the central pillar which is the super-fast elevator," he had directed. "You'll see the Care-Caster Room on the options. Choose that one and you'll go straight there."

It was as simple as that. Hector barked loudly and alarmingly throughout the entire, rapid, stomach-churning elevator ride, and Flair dropped all of her books on Dusty's toes. But they quickly reached the dizzying heights of the Care-Caster Room and stepped safely from the neat, cylindrical capsule. There were clear signs with small gold lettering indicating the Care-Caster Room, and Lost Property.

"We'll start with the Care-Caster Room," said Hugo.

"I think we all knew that, Hugo," said Henrietta. But she was not complaining. All of them, even Flair, were walking along the shiny, tiled, immaculately clean hallways with something approaching awe. The only other person in sight was a man, staggering slowly onwards in the direction they were going, with his back bowed low under the most enormous, ungainly load. They walked in silence, watching the man curiously, not knowing what to say or do to help him. And then Hector shattered the tranquillity around them.

"Hector!" reprimanded Zek. "Quiet, boy!"

Hector, whom Hugo had insisted should at least be on his lead, however much he disliked it, growled low in his throat, the hair standing high on his neck.

"I think...I think it's because of that *poor* man!" said Henrietta.

"I think we could probably deduce that, Henry," said Hugo drily.

"We ought to help him," said Timmy.

"That's so kind, Timmy," said Flair approvingly.

Henrietta tried not to giggle – which she invariably did at Flair's propensity to approve of Timmy, and at his to have absolutely no idea of her preference. One thing was sure: the man with the terrible burden certainly appeared to need help.

"Uh, excuse me, sir! Can we help?" asked Hugo, as they hastened to catch up with the man.

"Not too far to go now!" panted the man. "Just the next room on the right! If you would be so kind as to get the door..."

Dusty sprang to the massive double-doors labelled 'Care-Caster Room' and pushed the

solid, polished timbers aside. Into the room staggered the man with the burden, and all the Mustardseeds followed. Then the man did an extraordinary thing. He approached the gigantic pit which was sunk deep into the middle of the immense room; he went right to the very dangerous edge; then he flung the burden from him with all his might. Down went the burden – all the way into the bottom of the pit where there was a faint, hollow splash.

"That's better," said the man, straightening up and rubbing his back. "Some burdens are harder to bear than others! That one was a load, I can tell you!"

"It-it certainly looked like it!" said Dusty, amazed.

"Was it your burden?" asked Timmy.

The man shook his head. "I'm a Burden-Bearer," he said. "I help to bear other peoples' burdens. That's what the Bible says, isn't it? Bear one another's burdens[14]! I help people with burdens they can't bear."

"Wow!" said Dusty, "what an awesome job!"

"It's fulfilling the law of Christ," the man said simply.

"But what about all these?" asked Henrietta, as she observed the people dotted here and there around the vast pit. It was a sad sight. Some were weeping, some were moaning, some had sandwiches and flasks as if they habitually prepared for a day out here, some were merely glum, some were bitter and defiant. "What are they doing with their burdens? Why don't they throw them in?"

The man sighed rather sadly. "They're fishing," he said. "Some of them come every day; some people practically live here! The Care-Caster Room is always open to the public, you see. There's a way in from every home in Aletheia! These people want to cast their cares, like it says..." He gestured to golden lettering that glittered around the walls and sparkled in the reflection of the far away water down at the bottom of the Care-Caster pit. It said 'Casting all your care upon Him, for He cares for you.'[15]

"But why can't they let go of their cares?" asked Josie, pitying so many people in such a sorry state.

"They haven't learned to claim the promises of God," said the man. "They haven't accepted that they can cast all their anxieties and worries upon God, and they haven't asked for help from a Burden-Bearer. They just can't let go of their burdens! They throw them in on the end of a fishing line, and then sit there poking at them and reeling them back in again when the day is done. What they must do is hurl them into the pit without anything attached! And trust in God's care for them. Then, if their worries come again, they must constantly throw them into the bottom of the pit, not keep them on the end of a line!"

"What a shame," said Josie softly.

"I think they're a bit soft in the head," said Flair. "I once read…"

"It's been very busy recently," said the man, with evident concern. "More and more people arriving every day, and staying the whole day, just fishing with their cares! I think it's the Fretters that have got to them."

The children watched the very small, fly-like, puny creatures that buzzed around the people seated by the Care-Caster and even settled on their heads and shoulders.

"I'd like to come in here with some really strong bug-spray and kill them all!" exclaimed Henrietta.

"If only it was that easy," said the Burden-Bearer.

"But does this mean that these people aren't praying for other things, like the protection of Aletheia?" asked Timmy slowly. "That would mean they're wasting prayer time and energy, and fretting over their own troubles instead."

"That's it, Timmy!" said Hugo. "That's what we're meant to discover here!"

"We must add it to our prayer list," said Josie.

"I'm sure there must be something else we can do too," muttered Henrietta, thoroughly disgusted with the little buzzing bugs that pestered the people around the Care-Caster, even though many of them didn't seem to notice. "Some bug-spray or *something*!"

"That's the ticket!" said the man cheerfully. "And now, if you'll excuse me, the Burden-Bearer department is extra-busy just now. Burdens and cares everywhere! And in such glorious spring weather too!"

"What a nice man!" said Henrietta, when the Burden-Bearer left them.

The children contemplated the gloom of the folk fishing around the Care-Caster.

"Hector doesn't like it here," said Zek.

For once, Hector, who was seldom cowed by anything, lay compliantly in his young master's arms, with only a low-throated growl as proof that he was still an active participant in the Mustardseeds' activities.

They debated whether it was worth talking to any of the folk who sat silently contemplating their bundles of worries which hung at the end of their fishing lines. But what could they say? If these people didn't claim the promise in the Bible about casting care[15], why would they listen to children?

"Short of cutting their fishing lines, I'm not sure what we can do," said Hugo.

The Mustardseeds left the room quietly, unnoticed by any of the sad, preoccupied, unsuccessful Care-Casters present. They headed to the next door on the corridor.

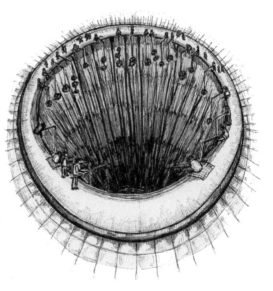

"I wonder what can possibly be kept in Lost Property," said Henrietta, as they reached that door. Dusty eagerly pushed it open.

"Wow!" they heard him murmur. "Absolutely awesome! I always wondered where the untargeted prayers went to! We can see incoming prayer on our Prayer Power Monitor – not the detail of course, we just assign the prayer to the right causes – but of course no one knows what to do with prayers that don't really mean anything! So we send them away down the underground network of pipes between the two Academies, and they must end up here, flying around the Lost Property Room!"

It was certainly an unusual sight. Hundreds of tiny pieces of paper whirling around and around the room, unable to rest – for they had no target – and so they flew until they were used up and exhausted; they hadn't been used purposefully at all.

"How awful!" said Henrietta, appalled. "Imagine all this prayer power going to waste! And just when we need prayer so badly too!"

"Hector! Down, Hector!" cried Zek, for, as much as Hector had disliked the previous room, this one had all the possibilities of a wonderful adventure with so many things flying around. Hector leapt into the air and snapped at a piece of paper, catching it neatly in his mouth.

Hugo took the paper from Hector. "Well, since he caught it, I suppose we can read it," he said. He opened it and read it while it lay fluttering helplessly in his hand. "Dear God, bless everyone, everywhere," he read.

"If only they'd put one name to it," sighed Dusty, "just one name! Or a description if they didn't know a name. Or even have someone in their mind! Then we could assign it properly and it would be some use!"

"I don't suppose there's much we can do about this room either," said Timmy gloomily. "I don't suppose there's any way we can re-assign these prayers as proper prayer power."

It was all rather depressing. Of course, they knew that in that vast, towering Academy, there were people doing great things, like the Burden-Bearers. But on their visit, the only things they had discovered were people weighed down by their own anxieties instead of turning to God in prayer, and wasted prayers flying around and around, not knowing where to land.

"The Meddlers must be enjoying themselves," said Timmy.

"And the Fretters too," said Hugo.

"Looks as if they're winning the war just now," added Dusty.

"You think prayer really matters, don't you?" asked Flair, as they left the Prayer Academy.

"Oh, it matters alright," said Hugo.

"Is it to do with the cross again?" asked Flair. "Is that the answer?"

Hugo looked ahead of them, to where the cross towered above the city of Aletheia. He had been taught the answer to that question from the time he could remember anything at all. "The cross is always the answer," he said.

CHAPTER 17
BACK AT THE BARN

Apart from their visit to the Prayer Academy, the Mustardseeds had by no means been idle, and they all had something to report at their next meeting, which was once more held in Mr Straw's barn. Hugo and Timmy, accompanied by a determined Flair, had carried out further research in The Outskirts of Aletheia, this time visiting people in DIY Crescent.

"I've always wanted to visit there," remarked Henrietta. "It looks so weird and interesting!"

"It certainly is," agreed Timmy.

"Yes, it is!" piped up Flair.

"The houses! Tell us about the houses," said Henrietta.

"That wasn't really the point of the exercise, Henry," said Hugo.

"Timmy?" appealed Henrietta. "Did you go inside one of the houses?"

"A couple of houses," conceded Timmy, who could never refuse a request from Henrietta. "They are pretty strange, just what they look like from the outside really. Like they've been built without anyone having any plans. Windows in strange places and all the wrong shapes, bits added where they shouldn't be, stuff like that. Some look like they're from another planet!"

"But what did the people have to say?" asked Josie, as usual poised with her pen at the ready. Flair quickly bent over her pad too.

Hugo sighed. "Well, this time, instead of people being distracted by how they should pray and waiting for new rules and regulations until they start praying – like the people in Law Villas – the people in DIY Crescent are inventing the oddest, weirdest ways to deal with Meddlers!"

"They're not praying about it at all as far as we could tell," said Timmy.

"That's right, Timmy!" said Flair.

Timmy didn't hear Flair. "They're completely caught up with

inventing ways to cope with Meddlers – detecting them, catching them..."

"We're trying to catch Meddlers too!" Zek whispered urgently to Jack.

"But I don't think these people are doing it to help," replied Jack. "Not like we are!"

"...Some of the folk at DIY Crescent are even *talking* to the Meddlers..." Timmy continued.

"Talking to them!" exclaimed Josie.

Hugo nodded. "They're selling 'Meddler Language Interpretation Kits' at the Shopping and DIY Centre," he said.

"You went to the Shopping Centre!" exclaimed Josie.

"As part of our research," said Hugo firmly.

"So, bottom line, they're not praying about the Meddler problem at all," said Henrietta.

"That's about it," said Timmy.

"What can we do about the folk in The Outskirts?" asked Dusty. "Anything at all?"

None of them could think of anything. If people drifted away from the cross, they forgot how much the Lord Jesus had done for them, and focussed on their own issues instead. And the Meddlers' plan of creating 'issues', and distracting people from praying, was so far proving horribly, easily successful.

"Well, I have some slightly better news, if that helps," said Dusty. "Shall I give my report?"

"You're next on the agenda," confirmed Josie.

"Right," said Dusty. "Well, bad news first, I guess, then some better news. I looked into the numbers of Rescuers absent from Aletheia on missions in Err. There are more Rescuers absent now than at any time since 1901 when there was a general revival. It's very unusual to have so many Rescuers absent from the city at once. And, get this! Most of the absences are categorised as 'Minor or Other Disturbances Requiring Aid'."

"Which sounds exactly as if it's due to Meddlers!" exclaimed Hugo.

"I suppose the adults are aware of this too?" asked Timmy.

"Oh yes," said Dusty. "They'll have loads of official information at their meetings. I think they know about it, and they probably know it's all because of Meddlers. But what can they do? Can they bring all the Rescuers back to guard fruit trees in Aletheia?"

Josie giggled faintly.

"No," said Hugo. "But it's like...we're all so helpless!" he exclaimed.

"But we're Mustardseeds!" said Zek.

"I know, Zek," said Hugo wearily.

But Zek didn't think Hugo got his meaning at all. He meant that even they, the smallest, least informed group in the battle against the Meddlers, could do impossible things if they had faith in God.

"What was the good news?" asked Timmy.

"Well, not exactly good, but better anyway," said Dusty.

"We'll take all we can get," said Hugo.

"Prayer power has slowly increased," said Dusty.

"Hurrah!" cried Henrietta.

"That's amazing," said Hugo. "I wonder who has started praying more now that wasn't before?"

"Well, we've got our group," said Jack. "Maybe others are doing the same."

"And Henry and I have been talking to important prayer warriors about how to pray more effectively," said Josie. "We're next on the agenda."

"Then it's us," whispered Jack to Zek. He stroked Fly's soft ears, then Hector's too. Somewhere in the proceedings, Hector, who had enjoyed an unusually busy day even by his standards – annoying Fly the collie, chasing a cat in the hay, digging a big hole in the middle of Mr Straw's garden, snapping at flies, and expending countless energy chasing up and down the fields waiting for the return of his young master – had actually fallen asleep. Jack and Zek had decided what to say in their update. They would say nothing of their mission to find the Meddler Pod, but they *could* share Mr Straw's concerns about the Fretters being trained to spread blight so that all the food supplies to Aletheia would be lost. That was surely important news!

Josie and Henrietta gave their report on finding out how to pray more effectively, which started with a visit to Mrs De Voté who they all knew ran the Faithful shop on the Fruit-of-the-Spirit shopping parade. Mrs De Voté had proved a great prayer warrior on a previous adventure[16], and Henrietta had not forgotten the lessons she had learned from the old lady.

"It's really like what we've learned about the mustard seed being one of the smallest seeds, and yet if we have faith which is placed in God, He can do impossible, incredible things, like He did in the purple storm![16]"

"Mrs De Voté says she prays because she knows that the God of Heaven answers prayer,[17]" said Josie. "We must pray believing that God can answer prayer."

"And we must pray according to the will of God," added Henrietta.

"What does that mean?" asked Jack, thinking that he and Zek had tried to do all of this, and yet God still hadn't answered their prayer about catching a Meddler and discovering the Meddlers' plan.

"It means that we must pray in keeping with what the Bible says about God," said Josie. "If we're praying in the will of God, then we know God *will* answer prayer![8]"

Jack thought about that. It was hard to know specifically whether finding the Meddler Pod was in the will of God. But God surely wanted the Meddlers' plans to be stopped...

"Mrs De Voté says that the strength of prayer is not in the person who is praying, but in God, Who is completely trustworthy," said Henrietta.

"But she mentioned Sanctification too," said Josie. "I think it must be important. Whiskers included it in his assignment too. Remember we were going to visit Sanctification and find out more about it? It's to do with being ready to be used by God, set apart to be used by Him, or something like that."

"Right," said Hugo. "Timmy and I will get on to that." They had been so busy elsewhere, that the trip Mr Mustardpot had recommended to Sanctification had always fallen down the list.

"Is it our turn now?" asked Zek. Like Hector, his day had been long and he was sleepy. He and Jack got up earlier these days, and packed every hour with farming, school, and their own research for the Mustardseeds.

"Yes, Zek," said Josie. "You and Jack are last on the agenda."

"Are you still doing research on Meddlers and Fretters?" asked Dusty with genuine interest.

Jack nodded. The scruffy folder, which went everywhere that the boys did, was once more present between them, currently squashed under Hector on their bale of hay. But it remained shut and the contents were a mystery to the rest of the Mustardseeds. "But we haven't quite finished that yet," he said.

"But we've got another update instead," said Zek.

"It's about Mr Straw's interview with Miss Communique," said Jack.

"Did they fall in love?" asked Flair with a giggle.

Jack thought that was a rather stupid comment, and Zek said, "I don't think that's a very good idea!" in such an indignant manner, that Henrietta and Josie giggled too.

"It's about a serious blight," said Jack. "All the food might be ruined."

"Did they really say that?" asked Hugo.

"It's Mr Straw's idea," said Zek.

"Oh," said Hugo, with evident relief.

"But it's very serious," said Jack. "Mr Straw thinks the Meddlers might be training Fretters to blight all the crops. Then if there's an invasion..."

"Yes," said Timmy. "That would be very serious!"

"But what can we do?" asked Hugo. "Apart from add it to our prayer list, of course!"

"And as we learned, prayer is everything!" said Henrietta.

"And we'll know all about Fretters soon too," whispered Zek to Jack. "We'll do more than pray!" And he patted the precious, scruffy folder which contained all their information – all about their enemies.

CHAPTER 18
OF MEDDLERS AND FRETTERS

Mr Straw was despondent. Zek and Jack, neither of whom was pessimistic by nature, both realised their friend was anxious, and they knew it was because he was worried about the future of the precious food crops of Aletheia. Every day the sun shone brightly; every day the green leaves and fragile new shoots grew and multiplied; yet Mr Straw watched the unfolding of this luxurious spring with unusual foreboding.

"It's because of the blight, isn't it?" asked Zek.

"There's something not quite right," said Mr Straw. "I can feel it in my bones. There's nothing I can prove to the Management Meeting in Aletheia. There are no fresh sightings of Green-Jacket Meddlers – which is suspicious in itself! But something is out there, just waiting to attack."

Of course, there was not much that Zek or Jack could say to comfort their friend. They knew, because they overheard the adults talking, that the main concern in Aletheia was about something called Team WondERRful which was coming to Aletheia, or close to it anyway. Neither Jack nor Zek was particularly interested in this. Zek said *Team WondERRful* sounded silly, and the two boys continued with their studious, careful research, focussing on Fretters instead of Meddlers. They continued their visits to Jude Faithful at the Judges' Academy. They copied notes and drew pictures. And their stained, scruffy folder, with two fresh, muddy paw prints of Hector's on the cover, bulged at the seams.

"Did you know that Fretters are actually *programmed* by Meddlers?" asked Jack. He had found that fact particularly interesting – and thought it had distinct possibilities too. "It's like there's a switch which makes them do things. This book that I'm reading says that Meddlers 'have sometimes been allowed to use Fretters to help them in their nef...uh...nefar-i-o-us work.'"

"Yes, Fretters are generally thought to be programmed and controlled by Meddlers, who are in turn controlled, or at least encouraged, by people in the land of Err," said Mr Straw. He stirred the porridge in the pan, enjoying the presence of his two young friends at his breakfast table, with their plots and schemes too. "Down, Hector," he said, ruffling the dog's ears. "You'll get your share when you lick out the pan!" Fly pushed up against Mr Straw, annoyed at Hector.

"Hector saves a lot of washing up," said Zek fondly.

Mr Straw laughed.

"But if Fretters can be programmed," persisted Jack, "then that means that if we happened, say, to catch one, we could *re-programme* it to do *other* things."

"Y-yes..." said Mr Straw slowly. "But you'd have to catch a Fretter *leader*. And that's like finding a needle in a haystack! The folk at the Academy say the Fretter leaders are the ones with the *instructions* inside them, and this is linked to all the thousands and even millions of Fretters who follow the leader. If you can change the leader's programme, they think you can change what *all* the Fretters do."

"We'll have to pray extra about that," remarked Zek.

"I think I did read about that somewhere," said Jack thoughtfully. "We've got an illustration of a Fretter leader somewhere too."

"And if you *did* catch a Fretter leader," said Mr Straw, intrigued with the idea, "how do you plan to re-programme it? No one has ever been known to do *that*!"

"We were thinking of that, weren't we, Zek?" said Jack.

"Yes," said Zek, taking a big spoonful of porridge. "You said your friend, the doctor..."

"Dr Pentone?"

"Yes, him. Well, he likes cutting up things and experimenting, doesn't he?"

"Yes, I think he does," said Mr Straw, amused at this description of his friend.

"And he's the cleverest man in Aletheia."

"He's probably that too," agreed Mr Straw.

"Well, then," said Zek, satisfied the answer was obvious. "He'll do it then!"

Mr Straw was always cheered by these conversations with the boys. Their faith might have been imaginative, but they had the simplicity to place it squarely and completely in God. They firmly believed that God could use them to help defeat the Fretters that Mr Straw thought might swarm across the farmlands of Aletheia at any moment. And Mr Straw was oddly comforted.

CHAPTER 19
SANCTIFICATION

Hugo and Timmy found that they didn't have to ask permission to visit the building called Sanctification. They asked Hugo's father, Hardy Wallop, about the possibility of a tour of the stone-pillared building at the corner of Redemption Square. They were surprised to find they were free to explore it whenever they wished.

"It's open to anyone at any time," said Mr Wallop. He didn't ask questions about this latest quest of the Mustardseeds; they didn't even know Mr Wallop knew who they were and what they were about. But he followed their investigations with quiet interest. He was very glad that these children were not taken up with the coming of Team WondERRful to recruit an Aletheian representative for the Revolting Nations Agreement. Indeed, the Mustardseeds had been too busy to pay it much attention.

"I wonder why we didn't explore here before," said Hugo, when he led the Mustardseeds, plus Flair and Hector, up the stone steps to the open, multi-pillared front of Sanctification. Etched above the pillars of the building were the words 'Set Apart by God'.

"Oh, is that what Sanctification means?" asked Dusty.

"That's similar to what Mrs De Voté said," said Josie. "Sanctification

– set apart."

"Set apart by God," mused Henrietta. "That's special."

The building was open and anyone could enter through the widely spaced pillars and investigate inside. But, open though it was, there was a feeling of secret treasures in the shadowy, echoing space. And despite the fact that a fresh breeze was blowing outside, not a breath of it reached beyond the pillars. There was not a speck of dust or the smallest petal of stray blossom on the shiny marble floor. The inside seemed untouched by the outside.

Once the Mustardseeds were beyond the pillars at the entrance, there were three options before them. These were three passageways, each entered through a stone archway. They all looked the same, apart from the fact that they bore a different name. They were simply called: 'Past', 'Present', and 'Future'.

"Which way shall we go?" asked Henrietta.

"Shall we start with *Past?*" suggested Timmy.

"Very logical," said Flair approvingly.

They ventured down the passageway named Past. And came to an abrupt halt.

"Oh," said Hugo. "That didn't take us far."

"It's blocked," said Josie, reaching out to touch the ancient timbers of the very sturdy door that stood before them. The door seemed moulded into the doorframe.

"There's not even a handle," said Jack.

"There's not even Bible access to enter either," added Dusty, feeling around the door for the book-shaped indentation which was the usual way to open locked doors in Aletheia. When a Bible was pressed on the door, people could enter.

"It says 'Private'," said Henrietta.

"Well, that's it then," said Hugo. "There's no way in."

"No way in?" said Flair. "Well, what's the point in that?"

"There's always a point to Bible truth," said Hugo.

"Perhaps that *is* the point," said Timmy thoughtfully.

"What?" asked Flair.

"The point is that it's meant to be kept hidden," explained Timmy. "Perhaps the Past of Sanctification isn't something we can know, or completely understand."

"Imagine being *set apart* by God in the past," said Dusty. "It's awesome when you think about it! It's like God chose us before we even knew about it!"

They turned and walked back to the entrance of the passageway, and headed towards the opening named 'Present'. This one quickly divided into two.

"'What You Are' and 'What You Do'," said Dusty, reading from the sign which labelled these two options.

They decided to split the options. Hugo, Dusty, Josie and Flair went through the open archway named 'What You Are' – and stopped abruptly in surprise.

"It's..." began Hugo.

"Awesome!" completed Dusty.

"Mirrors!" exclaimed Josie. She spun around in every direction, and no matter where she looked, it was the same; mirrors everywhere! It was not clear whether the room was square or round, or even large or small. There was no sense of proportion at all; just reflection. And then an even more surprising thing happened. Whatever their reflections might have been when they entered the room – and none of them could afterwards remember seeing what they were – when they stood still and looked in the mirrors, it showed a wonderful sight. They were clothed in robes of pure white; glistening, shining, perfectly clean; without any spot or blemish; washed and ironed in the most incredible washing cycle ever.

"It's..."

"Awesome!"

"Beautiful!"

It was hard to describe exactly how it felt to see yourself without any stains at all and realise that was *What You Are*.

"It must mean that this is how God sees us," said Josie in awe.

"When we are saved and washed clean![18]" said Dusty.

"I think God sees in us the Lord Jesus when He sees us like this," said Hugo.

"Doesn't the Bible say that the Lord Jesus is our righteousness?[19]" said Josie.

"God has set us apart to be something special for Him!"

"And He sees us like this!"

It was Josie who first noticed the muffled sob from Flair. They had been so taken up with their reflections, and the wonder of how clean God made them when He cleansed them from their sins, that they had forgotten Flair. Flair had never trusted in the Lord Jesus to put her sins away and make her clean. And, for the first time, they wondered what *her* reflection looked like in the mirrors. But one of the strange things about this room was that you couldn't see anyone else's reflection; they couldn't see what distressed Flair in the mirrors.

"Filthy dirty!" she cried. "Rags and tatters! What *is* this room? That's not *me*!"

"You're seeing yourself as God sees you," Hugo said as kindly as he could.

Josie tried to comfort Flair. Flair hadn't proved the most likeable girl with her quest for knowledge and her know-it-all attitude. But Josie remembered what it felt like when she saw her own reflection broken and shattered. She had thought she was beyond repair[1]. But then she had learned, that despite her rebellion and rejection, the Lord Jesus was still willing and able to make her whole again.

"It's because of the cross," Josie tried to explain to Flair. "The Lord Jesus can save you and make you clean and right!"

"It all comes back to the cross," sobbed Flair, quite distraught at her reflection. "That's what you told me, Hugo! The cross has all the answers!"

"Yes, it does," said Hugo.

"Even to this?!" wailed Flair, gesturing wildly at the reflection they could not see.

"Definitely," said Dusty emphatically. "God is great enough to clean up anyone! And when the Lord Jesus died He did enough to clean up every single person in the world and take away all their sins! You just have to trust Him to do it![6]"

"I'm going outside," said Flair. "I'll wait for you outside!" Her hand hid her eyes from the sight of her ruined reflection, and she almost ran, her satchel of books bumping around her, away from the revelation of what she truly was in the sight of God.

"I guess that's the consequence of not having the Lord Jesus to take your place and stand as your holiness," said Hugo soberly.

"I didn't think Flair cared too much about her appearance," said Dusty candidly, thinking of how untidy Flair often seemed. "She must have looked pretty bad to run away like that!"

"It must be the sight of how God views sin," said Josie. "How dirty and disgusting it must really be!"

Timmy, Henrietta, Zek and Jack had meanwhile entered through the open archway named 'What You Do' – and also stopped abruptly in surprise. They appeared to be standing before an immense swimming area. Crystal-clear water sparkled at their feet, gently lapping against the tiles. Around and about the walls there were mirrors; and dotted here and there were framed verses and instructions.

No one spoke, even Hector was quiet. They all wandered about the vast space, looking silently into the mirrors, reading the instructions on the walls, and watching the water moving and sparkling before them.

"The water in the, uh, swimming pool – or whatever it is – is the Water of Sound Doctrine," said Henrietta at last. She had flitted quickly around the room, skimmed over the writing and returned to the beautiful water, watching it with awe.

"I don't think it's exactly a swimming pool," said Zek doubtfully. "It says on the wall here about *washing away daily defilement*.[20]"

"It says something about separation," said Jack.

"Separation from sin and wrong things, to live a life pleasing to the Lord Jesus instead," said Timmy.

"So that's where the *set apart*[21] bit comes in, is it?" asked Henrietta. "It means to be separate?"

"Yes," said Timmy. "God has separated us and set us apart – for a purpose."

"Which is to be like the Lord Jesus," said Jack. "His representatives on earth.[11]"

"I think that's the Truth of Sanctification," said Timmy. "And *What We Do* is about how we live set-apart lives as Christians. It's like putting into practice what God has made us!"

"So, to be really useful as a Christian..."

"I think we have to be clean, every day; washed in the Water of Sound Doctrine; keeping apart from doing wrong."

"Then, when we're living clean, God can use us for great things!" said Zek. "That's why Mr Mustardpot wanted us to learn about Sanctification!"

"I think that must be it, Zek," said Timmy. "And if we're living lives set apart for God, we'll be focussed on what God wants us to be, and not be distracted by Err."

"I don't like my reflection in these mirrors," said Henrietta in a subdued voice. "I know I'm not completely clean."

"Nor I," said Timmy.

"Then we must all keep washing," said Jack. "Keep drinking and watering the Water of Sound Doctrine on everything we do."

"And then God can do something *really special* with us," said Zek.

The Mustardseeds, now minus Flair, didn't spend much longer

in the hallowed, appealing passageways of Sanctification. They felt concerned for Flair, although, as Dusty pointed out, there wasn't a better place for her to wait for them than in Redemption Square.

"Just a quick look through the Future passageway," said Hugo.

They all agreed. No one wanted to leave before they had seen what Future Sanctification was.

It was another room of simply mirrors. There were no features, no sense of large or small, or round or square, or of any perspective at all. And there were no reflections.

"Nothing," said Dusty, peering closely at the mirrored walls which were so mysteriously hiding their reflections.

"Stand still," said Hugo. "Look carefully..."

They were all still and watchful.

"Just faintly..."

"Yes, a faint shadow..."

"And words in the shadow..."

Silently, they all read the words, 'We shall be like Him'[22].

"It means like the Lord Jesus, doesn't it?" said Zek, as they left Future Sanctification and headed out to meet Flair.

"Yes, it means like Him."

CHAPTER 20
CLEAN

If it hadn't been for the increasing excitement that the Team WondERRful recruitment campaign was causing at school, the preoccupation and unsociability of the Mustardseeds might have been more noticeable. Their friends complained a bit, and a couple of the usual bullies, who weren't Christians, teased them and mocked them for being so 'religious', but they were mostly left alone. But not even the Mustardseeds, busy with their own agenda, could completely ignore the Team WondERRful event – which was coming right to the very boundaries of Aletheia. Somehow posters and leaflets appeared around the school. Never before had the affairs of Err penetrated the boundaries of Aletheia, right into the fiercely guarded domain of Mr Mustardpot himself. He was furious – but there was very little either he or the other teachers could do. As soon as the posters were torn down, more appeared to replace them.

Mr Mustardpot was understandably appalled, and when a new poster appeared all over the school announcing that the venue for the Team WondERRful campaign was to be the Turn-Aside Exhibition Centre, actually *inside* the boundaries of Aletheia, an emergency Management Meeting was hastily convened.

"Never, since the days of good Wiseman Steady, has such a thing been known!" roared the infuriated Mr Mustardpot to the important people assembled.

Of course, they were all as concerned as he was. Torn in many different directions by the rumours of the Meddlers, wondering where to put their resources, they all agreed that the Team WondERRful campaign must *not* be allowed to cross the Water of Sound Doctrine. It was too terrible to think that Err was invading Aletheia, coming so close to all they held dear, inviting any young person to join Team WondERRful and strengthen their ties with the dreadful land of Iniquitous.

"With the recent increase in prayer, we should have just enough power to raise the bridge across Unbelief Road and stop the entry of Team WondERRful; but we don't have prayer power to do much more than that," warned the Chief. "Are we all agreed this is the wisest thing to do?"

They were all agreed – with one exception. Poor, shy Mr Straw had to take a stand. "Is-is it possible," he faltered, surprising all those present, "that the Meddlers have managed this whole situation, so that we're looking in the wrong direction – while they attack something far more serious and with longer-lasting, devastating consequences?"

"You mean the crops, Croft," said Mr Mustardpot, knowing his friend's thoughts about the matter.

"Yes," said Mr Straw, "I mean our crops – all our supplies for the year ahead."

"It is a risk," said the Chief. "But in one night, could the Meddlers do so much damage, even if we weren't directing prayer cover to our food supplies?"

There was an outbreak of quiet discussion on the matter. Nearly everybody felt that, even if hoards of Meddlers did creep across the boundaries of Aletheia on the night everyone was focussed on the Team WondERRful event crossing into the city at Unbelief Road, still they surely couldn't blight *all* the future food of Aletheia.

"I don't deny the possibility of blight on our crops is very serious indeed," said the Chief, "but that's tomorrow's problem. Tonight we must protect Aletheia's boundaries!"

Mr Straw said no more. He hadn't explained his fear that the Fretters had been programmed to destroy the crops; it was only speculation on his part. But if that were true, and they lost their Pray-Always food supplies this year, they would be horribly weakened. The stores of food from the previous harvest were badly depleted from the particularly severe winter. If they didn't have enough safe food to harvest, there might be no tomorrow for Aletheia.

But Mr Straw had one surprising ally.

"I'm staying home and praying tonight, Croft," said Candour Communique. "Me and my friends – we'll be praying for the crops."

Candour walked slowly back through the city of Aletheia to gather her friends to pray for the safety of Aletheia and for the preservation of their precious food supplies. When she entered the tranquillity of Redemption Square, she was surprised to see the figure of a most untidy girl seated on the bottom step of the entry to Sanctification, in the corner of the square. She looked so utterly forlorn that Candour crossed the square to speak to her.

"Are you alright, dear?" she asked kindly.

"They said the answer was the cross, the answer is always the cross," said the girl. She peered at Candour through such dirty glasses that Candour wondered she could see at all. Then the girl pointed to the cross in the centre of the square, rising high above everything else around it. It wasn't a golden cross; it didn't sparkle with gems or look nice and glamorous. It was plain and stark and simple.

"I keep coming back here, but it doesn't seem to be the answer to anything at all!" said the girl. "But in there," she gestured to Sanctification behind her, "in there I'm so dirty and disgusting – there must be something to make me clean again!"

"Ah," said Candour. "You've been looking in the 'What You Are' mirrors in Sanctification, haven't you?"

The girl nodded. "I even tried praying to the cross," she said, "but when I went to check the mirror I was still filthy dirty!"

Candour nodded thoughtfully.

"So the answer can't be the cross, can it?" demanded the girl.

"The answer always lies at the cross," said Candour.

"That's what they said!"

"Who said?" asked Candour curiously.

"Hugo Wallop, and Timmy, and the others..."

"Are you one of the Mustardseeds?" asked Candour.

"Not really," said the girl. "I'm Flair Scholar. The Mustardseeds let me go to their meetings, but I'm not really like them at all. I just wanted to win the Importance of Sanctification and Prayer assignment."

"I see," said Candour.

"And now I don't care about the assignment at all," said Flair. "I mean, I think I already know why prayer is important – it's because of God."

"Exactly," said Candour. "Prayer is nothing if you're not praying to the right Person; but because God is able to do the impossible, when we pray to Him..."

"I know about that," said Flair impatiently. "But why, *why* am I still so unclean?"

"There is only one Person[23] who can clean away all your sin and make you right in the sight of God," explained Candour. "That's the Person of the Lord Jesus. It's no use trusting in symbols like the cross. Religion that focuses on *things* is no use at all. You need to trust the only Person who can make you completely clean again."

Flair was listening intently. "Then it's not the cross..."

"The cross is important because of what the Lord Jesus did there. He paid the debt we owed to God because of our sins; He paid enough so that every person in the world can be forgiven[6]! But not everyone is saved from their sins. You only become saved from the punishment for your sins and washed clean of them when you accept what the Lord Jesus did. When you ask Him to forgive you, what He did at the cross is put to your account. Then you are made clean and right in God's sight!"

"I just need to tell Him that?" asked Flair. "I just need to tell God that I want Him to forgive me and make me clean because of what the Lord Jesus has done for me?"

"That's all you need to tell Him."

Flair was quiet for some moments. She sat with her head bowed, murmuring softly. Candour didn't try to listen to what she said. She just waited. At last Flair raised her head and looked anxiously at the cross. "I did it," she said. "Did it work?"

"Shall we go and see?" asked Candour.

They walked through the forever calm and untouched passageways of Sanctification to the 'What You Are' mirrors and stood before them.

"Well, what do you see?" prompted Candour. But she didn't need to ask. The answer was in Flair's shining eyes, and she even removed her dirty glasses for a better look.

"Clean," she breathed. "Clean at last!"

CHAPTER 21
GUARDING THE CROPS

The night the Team WondERRful recruitment campaign was due to enter Aletheia was a very interesting one for all of the Mustardseeds. To start with, their distracted and concerned parents, summoned to pray at the cross for the raising of the bridge at Unbelief Road, to stop Team WondERRful from entering Aletheia, raised no objections to the Mustardseeds' late night meeting at Mr Straw's barn. The Mustardseeds assembled at the barn – all apart from Flair. Somewhere along the line Flair had disappeared and they had no idea that she had just met Candour Communique at Sanctification and become a Christian that very night. If Flair had disappeared at any other time Josie or Henrietta, or even one of the boys, might have remembered and tried to find her and include her, just to be kind. But this was like no other time in Aletheia. Great things were at stake, and Flair was forgotten.

The Mustardseeds had their own plans for the night of the crisis in Aletheia. Most of their school friends were planning to sneak away to the Turn-Aside Exhibition Centre, to see Team WondERRful making their speeches and having their show. It all looked so glitzy and glamorous on all the posters, and besides, there were lots of prizes and freebies promised. A few of the more rebellious students had even threatened to apply to be the representative of Aletheia!

The Mustardseeds were disgusted that any of the students from school would even consider being involved in something that, to them, went against all that Aletheia stood for. Hugo and Timmy did briefly discuss the solution of simply locking away all the kids that were potential candidates to represent Aletheia; but it was not really very practical. And besides, if it *were* possible, they decided that Mr Mustardpot would do that himself! But not even the adults could stand in the way of children choosing to join the other side.

In the end, Hugo and Timmy, and Henrietta and Josie, decided to watch the event from a safe distance. They would pray that the bridge over the Water of Sound Doctrine at Unbelief Road would rise, and that Team WondERRful would not be able to cross the boundary of Aletheia.

Dusty's task was different. He was heading into the Academy to the Central Control Room. He had 'borrowed' two Remote Talkers that were new at the Academy.

"They're still working on the technology," said Dusty, "but I think they'll do the trick!"

Dusty had one of the Remote Talkers, and Hugo had the other. Dusty planned to watch the Prayer Power Monitor in the Control

Room and report the state of prayer cover to the others. They would report to him what was happening. It was, they were certain, a good plan.

"I wonder if the adults have thought about doing that," said Josie.

"Oh, I expect so," said Dusty, who, being more aware of the intricacies of the Academy of Soldiers-of-the-Cross, had more confidence in the adults' foresight than the others generally did.

"Uh, what are you and Jack doing, Zek?" asked Hugo as they all prepared to leave for their 'mission'.

"We're guarding the crops," said Zek.

"Right," said Hugo. "All set? We'll meet back here at, let's say, 2200 hours."

Henrietta giggled. "You sound so funny when you're all *leader*-like and grown-up!" she said.

"I don't know why you have to say *leader* in that funny way, Henry," said Hugo.

"Because, sometimes you're just *funny* as a leader, that's why..."

Their voices grew distant as they set out eagerly to be part of the fate of Aletheia.

Jack and Zek, with the two dogs Fly and Hector, sat on in Mr Straw's barn.

They would watch the crops.

CHAPTER 22
THE STORM

To start with, no one noticed that the light had gone from the sky, or that dark storm clouds gathered thick and deep above and around Aletheia. There were no stars that night, but the four children who trekked across the Pray-Always Farmlands carried Bibles that shone brightly with light to show them the way[24]. They had gone prepared to face the foes of Aletheia. But they would not get too close, they would only watch and pray.

Through the dark of the brewing storm they could see the bright, coloured lights of Team WondERRful, with its many followers, approaching Aletheia. It was already more advanced than they had imagined it might be. They knew it was not just a simple matter of refusing entry or blocking the way: if it was, the Rescuers of the Academy of Soldiers-of-the-Cross would be there in their might. But when people didn't pray enough, when they were distracted like the people on The Outskirts, when the young Christians were all thinking about Team WondERRful, when the old Christians were anxious and being plagued with Fretters, when most forgot about guarding the Truth the city stood for – then nothing could stop the entry of the people of Err into Aletheia. What they needed was the mighty power of prayer to raise the bridge.

"They're almost at the crossing already!" said Henrietta. "The bridge is still down! The way is open!"

They hurried to the trees that crowded around the twisted route that was Unbelief Road. Was it already too late? Had Aletheia been invaded?

"I think this is as good a place as any," panted Hugo, finding a space for them beneath the tall, dark fir trees. "Dusty? Can you hear us?" Hugo held the Remote Talker to his mouth and pressed the 'talk' button as he spoke.

"Loud and clear!" came Dusty's cheerful tones. "I can see Team WondERRful on the Central Mission Detector. It's a red, flashing blob! I've never seen anything like it on the Mission Detector before; I don't think it likes it very much!"

"What about prayer power?" urged Timmy, leaning over Hugo.

"Prayer power should be sufficient," said Dusty.

"I think..." Timmy faltered and pressed suddenly against a tree.

"What?" asked Henrietta, alarmed at the look on Timmy's face.

"It's OK," said Timmy, and he laughed slightly sheepishly. "I think it was a Snare," he said.

Timmy had good reason to fear Snares. Once they had taken him captive; the frightening shadow creatures had bound him and carried him away[9]. But now that Timmy was a Christian he had no need to fear them. He could fight them with the Word of God.

"But what are *Snares* doing in Aletheia?" asked Josie, aghast.

"I expect they're coming with Team WondERRful," said Hugo.

"I think we probably knew it was something to do with Team WondERRful, Hugo," said Henrietta. "But I wish I'd put the rest of my armour on too! I just never thought we'd need our armour of God[13] inside the boundaries of Aletheia!"

"Uh, are you there?" Dusty's voice came over the Remote Talker.

"We're here," said Hugo. "There are Snares here too!"

"There are probably more creatures than Snares around you there," warned Dusty. "The Rascal Register is going crazy here!" They all knew he was watching one of the Control Room's fascinating machines that captured all kinds of information about the creatures of Err, where they were and what they were up to.

"What's that sound?" asked Hugo, alarmed at the screech that sounded through the Remote Talker.

"It's the Aletheia Alert!" said Dusty. "I've never heard it sound before! I don't even know how it works and none of the rest of the team are here! They're all with the other adults, praying at the cross!"

"Well, I think they all know there's an alert in Aletheia anyway," said Timmy reasonably.

Henrietta giggled faintly. She had crept close to Hugo and her arm was linked firmly through Josie's. This wasn't exactly what they had expected. They had thought merely to watch the lights and sights of Team WondERRful, and hopefully to see it turn back from the boundaries of Aletheia. Instead they felt the presence of wicked creatures that were the enemies of Christians. It felt like they were under attack in the land of Err, not safely within Aletheia's boundaries.

"Uh, you probably don't want to know this," said Dusty through the Remote Talker.

"Go on," said Hugo. "We may as well know what we're up against."

"The Storm Tracker is filling with smoke. There's a storm – and it's about to hit Aletheia!"

At Dusty's words, only just completed in time, the most terrifying crash of thunder shattered the quiet of the forest around them.

Josie stifled a scream and Henrietta clutched her. Hugo and Timmy were no less startled; they were just determined not to show it.

"We should have stayed near the cross," cried Hugo, above the next immense roll of thunder.

"But we came to pray about…!" Henrietta's words were drowned in the crackle of lightning which suddenly dazzled them and the resounding roar of thunder which followed.

"I think Hugo means we could have prayed better near the cross," said Timmy. "We would have been able to see the whole thing happening from the foot of the cross, and been safe there too!"

"I thought it would be better to be close to the action," said Henrietta.

"I know," said Hugo. "We all made that mistake."

"Well, it's not too late," said Josie, starting to shiver as rain began to pelt them through the trees. "Let's go back to the cross!"

The storm was so violent, the rain so heavy, that they could barely see what was happening at the crossing into Aletheia.

"All OK?" came Dusty's voice over the Remote Talker.

"Heading back to the cross," said Hugo.

"Good idea," said Dusty. "I think folk must already be praying there, prayer power is up!"

That, at least, was cheering. They stuck close together as they hurried back across the suddenly drenched fields, guided by the cross that even now showed clearly through the storm. They were wet to the skin, cold with the sudden chill of rain, blasted with thunder, and terrified of the crackle of lightning. But the closer they got to the cross, the safer they felt. The cold presence of Snares was left behind them. The Stumbles that Hugo was certain were carpeting the forest floor, slowing their footsteps, were not on the streets of Aletheia. And at the cross were gathered the great and small of the city, focussed on the west, anxiously watching the bridge over the Water of Sound Doctrine. Was the prayer sufficient? Would the bridge rise and stop their enemies from crossing the boundary and entering the city of Truth? There was always calm at the cross, and praying was easiest there. But the crowd that watched were anxious nonetheless.

The first lights of Err reached the crossing.

The rain lashed the procession and obscured the view. The watchers at the cross were silent.

Henrietta clutched Hugo's arm.

Slowly, and then with increasing momentum, the bridge began to rise.

Without that bridge, the Water of Sound Doctrine could not be crossed.

Team WondERRful could not enter!

There was a shout of triumph from around the cross. It was a small victory in a much bigger war, but they felt it was a victory nonetheless. There was talking, and even laughter, as people dispersed. The night's work was over.

"Hello? Hello?" Dusty's urgent tones were lost in the happy babble of the night's victory. "What's happened? Hugo? Timmy? Are you there? What's happened to the prayer cover? It's gone right down! Has everyone stopped praying?!"

After a while, Dusty gave up trying to get through on the Remote Talker. He could see very clearly on the huge Mission Detector screen in the Control Room that the bridge was raised. He supposed that the four Mustardseeds, who had seen Team WondERRful stopped from entering Aletheia, had returned to Mr Straw's barn for their late rendezvous. He wondered if he should go there too.

But something told him he should stay.

He slumped wearily by the Rascal Register. He was the only one left in the Control Room. He would watch and pray as long as he was able.

That night, thousands and millions of Fretters were carried on the wings of the storm over the boundaries of Aletheia, coming to rest amongst the crops and trees. They were there at the bidding of their masters, the Meddlers. They were programmed with only one purpose:

At the first light of morning, they would attack the food supplies of the city of Truth.

Then Aletheia could be destroyed.

CHAPTER 23
THE FRETTER

Jack and Zek kept watch in Mr Straw's barn. They didn't know about the victory at the crossing of the Water of Sound Doctrine; they didn't know that the bridge at Unbelief Road was raised, and that Team WondERRful had been stopped. They sat in the barn and listened intently to each night sound. Their careful, painstaking research into Fretters and Meddlers had taught them that Fretters made a faint buzzing sound. They were certain they would hear if those destructive creatures came, as Mr Straw feared, to destroy the crops.

But when the first crash of thunder shook the barn, the ferocious storm drowned out the sounds of the night, and, with it, all hope of Jack and Zek hearing the arrival of the Fretters. The two boys could only huddle close together in the barn, with Hector terrified and shaking between them, and Fly the collie pressed close to Jack's side. The only thing they could do was wait for the storm to pass. It did pass, however, and then they ventured out of the barn and took stock of the rain-soaked fields and the dripping trees. Hector was more than glad to be free. He had hated the crashing thunder and sizzling lightning, but when it was over he forgot about how frightening it had been, and scampered happily away from the barn to see if any careless rabbit had wandered too far from its hole and was up for a night chase.

At first, it seemed to Zek and Jack, as they walked through the fields close to the barn, that the dripping trees and waving grass was just the result of the storm. There were night sounds, but they were perhaps normal night sounds. The hoot of an owl; the snuffle of the newest calf in its pen with its mother; the faint sound of insects...

"Does that buzzing sound like a bee?" whispered Zek to Jack.

"It can't be a bee," said Jack. "I don't think they come out at night."

They moved slowly to the nearest tree, peering up into its branches. The branches and twigs and new leaves were wavering and moving oddly, as if bowed with a load they did not wish to bear.

Zek reached as high as he could up the tree and poked hard at a small knob on the branch. "Ow!" He snapped his hand quickly back and jumped away from the tree.

"What was it?" Jack asked breathlessly.

"It bit me!" exclaimed Zek.

"A-a Fretter?" asked Jack, aghast that their worst fears might actually be true after all.

"It must have been," said Zek, holding his finger. "What else...?"

They didn't know what else might be lurking amongst the fresh buds of the fruit tree; but they did know that Fretters could bite. They had two tiny, nasty, needle-sharp fangs. They had read about it in one of the musty books that Jude Faithful had unearthed for them. There had even been a picture of a Fretter bite which Jack had painstakingly copied out.

The boys examined the small bite on Zek's finger in the light of their Bibles in the barn. They looked at their faint copy of the picture of a Fretter bite; then back at Zek's finger again. There seemed to them no doubt about the matter. The two tiny incisions on his finger meant Zek had been bitten by a Fretter!

They left the barn again to look at the sagging trees, at the weird waving of the grass, at the drooping fresh green shoots. If they looked very, very carefully they could faintly discern the horrid, bulbous shapes of thousands and millions of clutching Fretters. Many as small as a fly, they sat on blades of grass, on shoots of oats, wheat and barley, on potato leaves, on every green sign of life in vegetable patches, and on every precious new bud in the fruit trees. They were still, and almost silent, apart from the barely detectable buzzing that seemed to have been muted or muffled, perhaps by design. The Fretters were ready and waiting to attack.

Jack and Zek walked across fields and through orchards, just to make doubly-triply sure. But it was the same everywhere they turned. There could be no doubt about any of it.

"W-what shall we do now?" asked Zek.

The boys had come prepared for several contingencies. They had prayed most sincerely about helping to stop the Fretters, and firmly intended to be a part of it. They had just never anticipated, in their wildest dreams, the horror of hoards of Fretters that were far, far beyond the capabilities of two small boys, if not already beyond all the combined might and power of Aletheia.

"We'll use our jar," said Jack decisively. "The first thing is to catch one. Then we'll have to get Mr Straw and show him."

"Right," said Zek.

Both boys hesitated. For very obvious reasons neither of them particularly wanted to handle a nasty, angry Fretter, and stick him in a glass jar. The gloves they had had the foresight to bring with them belonged to Mr Wallop; but they now knew the gloves were far too big to handle a Fretter.

"I'll do it," said Jack bravely. Zek already had a very nasty bite on his finger, which was swelling and turning a weird shade of green.

"Are you sure?" asked Zek, sounding very relieved.

"It's fine," said Jack stoically. He removed an empty jam jar, borrowed from Mrs Wallop's store, from the rucksack he was carrying. He removed the lid...

And suddenly they were in the middle of the most terrific commotion!

Hector, followed closely by Fly, flung himself upon them – a small, scruffy, white bundle; frantically excited; covered in damp soil; smelling vaguely of farm manure; with straw and twigs and unidentified paraphernalia strewn about him...and something buzzing strangely in his mouth.

"A-a-a..." Zek could barely catch his breath, as well as catch Hector, and avoid Fly who was leaping most indignantly at Hector and clearly wanted the buzzing creature for herself.

"F-f-fretter...!" stammered Jack. He flung himself into the fray and grabbed wildly at the buzzing, biting creature that was hanging from a wing in Hector's mouth. Zek valiantly tried to restrain Hector, and Fly continued to try and grab the Fretter.

It was touch and go for a while whether Hector or Fly would just swallow the creature. It was larger than the tiny fly-like Fretters they could discern all around them, and it was clearly extremely angry. Hector, not enjoying the sensation of being bitten by small, razor-sharp fangs, and not enjoying the taste of the wing of the Fretter, was trying to eject it from his mouth. Fly, obviously thinking the Fretter was her property, snapped at the Fretter. The Fretter used tiny claws and appeared to be punching as well as biting Hector and Fly, and then, to his own considerable surprise, Jack had the Fretter in his hands.

The Fretter was surprisingly heavy and solid, with hide that felt like spiky armour. It was not a pleasant feeling, and the creature sank its nasty teeth into his fingers and thumb again and again.

Somehow Jack hung on. He got the Fretter to the jar and shook it until the creature fell in a heap at the bottom. Then, quick as a flash, Jack put the lid on the top of the jar. The Fretter rushed frantically to the top and hit its head on the lid with a thump; it slumped down to the bottom again.

"We got him! We got him!" cried Zek in triumph.

"We got him," said Jack wearily. His hands were stinging like crazy but the next moment he forgot all about that. Hugo's voice was calling faintly from the barn.

"Zek? Jack? Are you out there? Is everything alright?"

When Jack and Zek arrived back at the barn, the news that the other Mustardseeds had thought so important faded into utter insignificance. There was a short period of complete chaos as Hugo, Timmy, Henrietta and Josie exclaimed at the state of the two younger boys, and Jack and Zek tried to explain exactly what had transpired.

They all stared solemnly into the jar at the large Fretter who was still looking rather stunned, and extremely grumpy.

"I knew Hector could do it," said Zek happily. "We read about a dog catching a Fretter in 1928, didn't we, Jack? Then we just knew Hector could do it!"

"I think Fly might have caught it first," said Jack cautiously, remembering Fly's indignation that Hector had stolen her prize. The two dogs capered happily around the children. They seemed none the worse for the Fretter bites they had both suffered, and Fly clearly still wanted to deal with the Fretter.

"Your finger, Zek!" exclaimed Henrietta, "and Jack! Oh, Hugo! Look at Jack's hands!"

Jack's hands were indeed a sight to behold. There were numerous nasty two-fanged bites that were already swelling and turning the same sick green colour as Zek's bite. And Zek's bite was now starting to weep strange, pea-coloured pus.

"We need to get you both to the doctor at once," said Josie.

"We need to see Mr Straw first," said Zek. "We must show him the Fretter."

"We can take the Fretter to him," said Hugo kindly.

But nothing would move Jack or Zek on this point. "It's because we know about Fretters, Hugo," said Zek most earnestly.

"There's something about *this* Fretter," said Jack. "It's very important!"

CHAPTER 24
POISONED!

At some point during that night of horrors and heroism, Mr Straw had dozed off. He had been praying, and praying, and praying. But long hours of anxiety and despair had made him tired, and when there was loud knocking at his door he suddenly awoke and found himself kneeling by his bed. He felt strangely refreshed and at once rushed down the stairs to the front door, wondering what fresh calamity might be upon the farmlands.

Hugo Wallop was on his doorstep.

"You kids are still here?" asked Mr Straw in surprise. "I thought you must have gone home hours ago!"

"Mr Straw," said Hugo, without preamble, "please could you come to the barn, sir? Zek and Jack have caught a Fretter and we need your help."

Mr Straw stuck his feet into the nearest pair of wellies and, without further question, went with Hugo to the barn. He thought he would never forget the sight of the two small boys, dishevelled, dirty, damp, with their hands swollen and weeping from Fretter poison, and a large Fretter in a jar on the floor of the barn, buzzing extremely angrily.

"They came, Mr Straw!" said Zek.

"They're everywhere," said Jack. "Millions of Fretters all over the crops!"

Mr Straw nodded grimly. Even in his walk to the barn he had been aware of the peculiar, faint vibrating in the air. His worst suspicions were confirmed.

He knelt down by the boys. "We need to get you to Dr Pentone," he said, looking at their hands. And their faces too. Their faces were losing their healthy colour; they were decidedly pasty and green-tinged.

"We need to take the Fretter to him anyway," said Zek.

"Look, Mr Straw," said Jack, and he carefully lifted the mean, angry Fretter up between his swollen hands. It raged and banged its tiny claw-like fists against the glass jar; it jumped up and down, knocking its head against the lid of the jar again and again. "We think it might be the *leader*," said Jack solemnly.

Mr Straw stared at the creature in the jar incredulously. He had followed the boys' research, and done plenty of his own. He knew the distinguishing marks of a Fretter leader.

Could it really be? Was there even the smallest chance that the wicked, angry creature trapped by two small boys could hold the key to saving Aletheia...?

Dusty kept watch in the Control Room by the Rascal Register machine. It wasn't making any sense. He had never taken much notice of the Rascal Register, which was set in a corner and usually ticked over quite contentedly. It churned out reports for Rescuers in the land of Err, about the presence of the creatures of Err and their activities in the various Regions. But the ticking got louder and louder, the little needle that recorded numbers and trends became quite violent in its movements, and the ticker-tape it churned out was now coming so rapidly and with so many squiggles that it was filling up the corner of the Control Room. Dusty didn't know how to work this machine. But something was clearly wrong. And when the Aletheia Alert machine sounded loudly for the second time that night, Dusty pressed the emergency alarm button. The Aletheia Alert machine was glowing red-hot, and the dial showed 'Imminent attack'; it was definitely time to call for help.

Captain Ready Steadfast suddenly loomed reassuringly on the Observer Deck above the Control Room. He picked up a speaking tube from the balcony. "Are you on your own down there, son?" he asked.

"Uh, yes, sir, sorry to disturb you, sir," said Dusty. "Uh, it's the Aletheia Alert, sir..."

But there was no need to explain. Captain Steadfast took one look at the glowing machine, which appeared to be ready to explode at any moment, and began barking commands into the speaking tube to people all around the Academy.

Dusty slumped against the nearest machine in relief. His work was over at last. The crisis now lay in the capable hands of someone else.

Jack and Zek remembered very few of the details of that strange night following the capture of the Fretter. After locking Hector and Fly in the house, Mr Straw crammed all the children and the glass jar containing the angry, buzzing Fretter, into his farm Atob and roared across the rain-drenched fields, crushing Fretters left, right, and centre as they went.

Mr Straw's Atob was a three-wheeled vehicle, similar to other Atobs in the wider land of Err, but with huge sturdy wheels that simply ate up the land beneath them. Usually it was used slowly and methodically in farm work. But tonight the Atob rushed across fields, through orchards, and even through the manicured lawns of the Judges' Academy, leaving three distinct, muddy tyre-marks in the soft grass. Mr Straw merely muttered, "Desperate times call for desperate measures," and didn't seem to care about the tyre-marks at all. Neither did any of the others. Jack and Zek were clearly very sick and their colour was worsening. They needed to get to the hospital wing of the Academy of Soldiers-of-the-Cross, and Mr Straw took all the short-cuts he could to get there as soon as possible.

Dusty's Remote Talker devices proved more than helpful in this latest emergency. Hugo radioed Dusty – who was still in the Control Room – and Dusty sent an emergency message to Dr Pentone. So, by the time the small party of Mr Straw, Mustardseeds, and buzzing Fretter arrived, Dr Pentone and a small team of assistants were waiting at the hospital entrance of the Academy. And with them was Dusty.

None of the Mustardseeds, including Dusty, had ever been into the hospital wing of the Academy before. Another time it would have been fascinating to them – to see the laboratories, and offices, and wards, and strange locked rooms of Dr Pentone's domain. But now they rushed through it all, following the decisive figure of Theo Pentone himself – who took one look at Zek and Jack and rapped out rapid orders to his staff. Henrietta clung to the small boys, tears running down her face at their damaged hands, tightly shut eyes, and strange, vomit-green faces.

"They'll be quite alright," said Dr Pentone, calmly and firmly. "They won't suffer much harm from the blight-poison. It's intended for plants, not small boys. I've got the very thing to treat them. Just leave them with us."

Zek opened his eyes. "Is it...is it really a Fretter leader?" he muttered.

Dr Pentone smiled grimly. "I do believe it is," he said. "You boys might save Aletheia yet!"

Zek smiled. His eyes slid shut again. And then he and Jack were carried from their sight.

CHAPTER 25
DISARMED

Dr Pentone left the two boys in the care of his staff and led the others into a most interesting room. The Mustardseeds gazed around them in horrified fascination, looking at the strange specimens on the shelves in Dr Pentone's 'Experimentation Laboratory'.

"Theo enjoys cutting things up," said Mr Straw rather drily.

"This is where I like to cut up children in my spare time," said Dr Pentone, winking at them. "Any time you'd like to volunteer…"

They all laughed. They were so relieved that Zek and Jack were apparently going to be alright. And, even now, through the heroism and mustard-seed-faith of these two small boys, Aletheia might yet be saved from the attack of millions of waiting Fretters. If Dr Pentone could re-programme the Fretter leader, then all the millions of waiting Fretters, who were linked to the leader, would be re-programmed automatically too. There was just the smallest chance that all the Fretters could be stopped from blighting the crops.

But time was against them.

Ticking away into the night.

And every precious second counted.

"I wonder why the wretched creatures haven't started attacking the crops already," mumbled Dr Pentone, carefully setting down the now-berserk Fretter in the jar on the middle of his long, white table. "Do you know why that is, Croft?"

"My guess is that the Meddlers can't programme the Fretters for two things at once," said Mr Straw. "It seems to me they have been programmed for silence at night, although they still emit a very faint buzzing. Once morning comes, the programme probably changes from 'Silence' to 'Destruction'."

"Makes sense to me," said Dr Pentone. He was bending closely over the glass jar, looking carefully at the leaping, raging, furious Fretter. "He's a leader alright," he confirmed. "His size…"

"And the markings on his legs…"

"And…uh huh! That's the ticket…I can see his programme switch, Croft! Just as you said! Quite incredible! What a shame I don't have time to make sketches and notes…"

"No time for that," said Mr Straw anxiously. He was thinking of the crops, and the evil that was poised, waiting to destroy them.

"Can you reset the programme?" asked Timmy.

"Well, it's never been done in Aletheia before, as far as I'm aware," said Dr Pentone, "but it's our only chance of stopping their attack in the morning. So you'd all better pray that we can."

They all watched silently, with bated breath, as Dr Pentone put on gloves and held tiny wires against the jam jar lid. Blue sparks collided and shot down the side of the jar, and the Fretter inside once more slumped to the bottom, stunned and dazed.

"He's not having a very good night, is he?" asked Timmy.

Henrietta giggled wearily.

"Serves him right!" said Josie. "When I think of poor Zek and Jack...!"

Mr Straw peered at the helpless-looking creature. "It's incredible that something that small..."

"Can do something so big," completed Dr Pentone. "But it's the first thing we should remember."

"It applies to us too, doesn't it?" remarked Dusty. "Like Jack and Zek..."

"The faith of a mustard seed," murmured Dr Pentone, taking a tiny scalpel and probing the back of the Fretter. "Yes, see here, Croft? The programme switch!"

Sure enough, an almost microscopically small switch was revealed under the armour-plated skin of the Fretter. Dr Pentone got out his most powerful microscope and set the Fretter on the plate. He put strange goggles over his eyes. They made him look even more like an eccentric scientist. He peered through the lens. They all kept extremely still and silent, as if the least movement might disrupt his work. He held a small wire and probed the minute device built into the back of the Fretter. It was a series of wheels and cogs and wires, so small you couldn't see them all without magnification. At last, he removed a tiny top.

"Five programme settings..." they heard Dr Pentone say in an undertone. "I wonder..."

With steady precision the doctor moved the tiny wire, and there was a small, discernible *click* in the silence of the laboratory, followed by sudden, frantic ticking.

"Watch closely now," said Dr Pentone, "but don't get too close..." He stepped hastily away from the table, his strange goggled eyes fixed intently on the unhappy Fretter leader. And then,

POP!

The Fretter leader exploded in a puff of sick, green smoke! There was the awful stench of very rotten eggs and they all watched in astonished silence as the green smoke cleared to reveal the smouldering remains of the Fretter leader. Dr Pentone didn't move. He held up his hand for silence as the children began to talk in excitement. And, through the stillness of the night, through the thick walls of the Academy, they all heard faint popping...pop, pop, pop...like the exploding of wet fireworks. Then, at last, Dr Pentone smiled.

"It's done," he said. "It really worked! The Meddlers have built in a 'Self Destruct' option on the Fretter leader, presumably in case they go wild or they lose control of them." Slowly he removed the strange goggles from his eyes.

"And the others – they're all dead too?" asked Josie.

"That was the popping in the night," said Mr Straw.

"They all exploded! Just like that!" exclaimed Dusty.

Dr Pentone nodded. "Whatever happens to the leader, happens to all the followers too," he said. "If you tackle the root of a problem, very often you tackle the whole problem. I don't know what mess there will be on your crops though, Croft," he added wryly.

"But at least we'll live to fight another day!" said Mr Straw. "And there's nothing the Water of Sound Doctrine can't clean away!" He wrung his friend's hand. "Good work, Theo!" he said.

"Good work, kids!" said Dr Pentone.

"Well done, Zek and Jack!" said Henrietta.

"And now to get to another emergency Management Meeting!" said Dr Pentone. But this one they did not mind. For, at last, they had good news.

The Mustardseeds, minus Zek and Jack who were staying in hospital overnight, were going home. The sun was peeping over the horizon. At last the long night, for them at least, was at an end. Another small victory had been won for Aletheia. They watched Mr Straw and Dr Pentone walk briskly down the corridor, carrying the glass jar containing the still-smouldering Fretter. They were heading to the Management Meeting – which had been convened by Captain Steadfast after Dusty sounded the emergency alarm in the Control Room.

"I wonder if Mr Straw has remembered he's wearing his wellington boots," remarked Josie.

And then they all looked at Dr Pentone.

"I don't think anyone will notice Mr Straw's boots," said Henrietta.

For Dr Pentone, happily swinging the precious jar, was wearing bright-red, tartan slippers.

There was a weary, strained silence in the massive Management Meeting room when Dr Pentone opened the door. He was inclined to enjoy dramatic gestures, and he swung the glass jar up before the assembled group of extremely tired managers. Of course, the explaining of exactly what had transpired took longer than that, but in the first gesture, everyone there realised that the almost impossible had been accomplished and Aletheia had been saved.

Candour Communique, exhausted by her night of prayer, thoroughly enjoyed this unforeseen, unexpected victory. It was made all the more memorable by the sight of Croft Straw in dirty wellington boots, with eccentric Dr Pentone in incredibly bizarre-looking slippers that he clearly didn't know he was wearing. She was touched when Croft Straw went out of his way to speak to her. "Thanks for praying," he said gruffly.

She nodded. Both of them realised how much the triumph of this hour belonged to those who had faith only the size of a mustard seed – placed firmly in a very great, all-powerful God[25].

Mr Hardy Wallop leaned forward in utter astonishment to examine the glass jar which contained the smouldering Fretter. Upon it, in his wife's handwriting, were the words 'Strawberry Jam'. But within the jar, very definitely, was a dead Fretter leader. Mr Wallop gathered as much of the explanation as he could, and hurried off to the hospital wing of the Academy to see two small boys, the heroes of the hour, now peacefully sleeping off the effects of blight-poisoning.

But when he reached the room, only one boy was there.

Jack Merryweather was gone.

CHAPTER 26
FLAIR'S CONFESSION

"Dad?" Zek opened his eyes to find his father, Mr Hardy Wallop, seated at his bedside. His head felt heavy and slow, like he was waking from a very long and complicated dream. Across the comfortable room he could see other beds – all empty; a nurse in the uniform of the Academy of Soldiers-of-the-Cross was watering some spring flowers close by. Weirdly enough, everything he looked at seemed to be a rather sickly shade of green.

"How are you feeling?" Mr Wallop asked his son.

"Are you green?" asked Zek distinctly.

Hardy Wallop shook his head with a smile. "I think that's still the effects of the blight-poisoning," he said. "Dr Pentone said you might feel a bit peculiar for a few days. That's quite an adventure you've had!"

"I don't think we exactly broke any rules," said Zek, struggling to recall any misdemeanours he might have committed in his dealings with the angry, poisonous Fretters.

"No one is worried about broken rules," said Dad reassuringly. "You and Jack saved the day! That Fretter you caught...well, through it Dr Pentone managed to destroy all the Fretters. The crops are saved!"

"We did it?" said Zek wonderingly. "It actually worked? We prayed that it would..." He stopped suddenly, and sat up in the bed and looked around. "Where's Jack?" he asked. But as he asked it, he already knew. "He went away again, didn't he?" he said.

"Yes," Dad said quietly. "I think Jack Merryweather has gone home."

Zek sank back against his pillows again. "I wish he didn't have to go," he said.

Dad nodded understandingly.

"How did he go?" asked Zek. Mr Wallop, as Superintendent of Entry to Aletheia, was the Aletheian expert on entry to and exit from the city. If anyone knew the answer, it was him. But there were still sometimes unexpected doorways to and from Aletheia into another land, and Jack Merryweather seemed pretty good at finding them.

Hardy Wallop considered what to say. "Whichever way he went, I think he'll find the way back," he said.

Meanwhile, the city was focussed on the clear up arising from the victory over the Fretters – who had been utterly destroyed. They had exploded and imploded and there wasn't a single, pesky buzzing creature left across the Pray-Always Farmlands of Aletheia. But it wasn't very nice on the farmlands. Dead Fretters, with horrible green poison oozing from them like bogies, left sticky goo on everything. The beautiful new green, the tender crops, the fresh new buds, were all sadly dirty and defiled. But across the Pray-Always fields Zek could see large Atobs working, spraying the cleansing Water of Sound Doctrine on everything. Mr Straw waved at him from his Atob, charging up and down the fields with water going everywhere. Fly the collie sat pressed up against him, pleased with her vantage point. Ahead of him, flying like a speck of dirty-white through the Fretter-goo, came Hector, barking loudly with joy.

Zek scooped up Hector and pressed his face into his messy coat with deep content. He missed his friend, Jack. And he thought Hector probably missed Jack too. But he had their precious folder intact. He would do his best to represent Jack at the meeting of the Mustardseeds.

Hugo called the meeting to order as Zek handed out the fresh lemonade Mr Straw had made for them that morning, before he went to clean his fields with the Water of Sound Doctrine.

"Uh..." Hugo cleared his throat. "First business this morning is that Flair would like to make an announcement," he said.

"Oh," said Josie. "You might have told me that, Hugo. I could have altered the agenda!"

"That's alright," said Flair quickly, "it won't take long."

Zek handed Flair a glass of lemonade and she set it down on the barn floor. Zek thought it was just as well that Flair didn't notice when

Hector quickly sampled her drink. Instead, Flair looked distracted.

"It's only that-that I'm one of you now," said Flair.

"Right," said Hugo, rather puzzled. "Well, you've always been, uh, welcome to our meetings..." Hugo trailed off uncertainly, wondering how honest that was.

"No," said Flair, "what I mean is that I *believe*! I believe what you believe! I'm a *proper* Mustardseed!"

"No kidding!" exclaimed Dusty.

"You mean – you've become a Christian?" said Henrietta.

"Yeah," said Flair. "*That's* what I mean!"

"That's great, Flair," said Timmy.

Flair blushed and looked pleased.

"That's really great," added Hugo.

"Awesome!" said Dusty enthusiastically. "Just awesome!"

"Does that mean you'll like Hector now?" asked Zek.

Flair chose to overlook that question, and Zek didn't think Hector's cause would be helped should Flair discover why her lemonade glass was now half empty. She didn't seem to notice, however: she took an absentminded sip and then returned the glass to the barn floor again.

"How did it happen, Flair?" asked Josie, unable to resist taking notes even about this.

"I kept visiting Sanctification," said Flair.

"Did you really?" asked Dusty.

"And I kept seeing how dirty and awful I was in the sight of God. But then I met Candour Communique in Redemption Square and she explained how I needed to trust in the Person of the Lord Jesus, and not in a symbol like the cross."

"Awesome!" said Dusty.

"So that's what I did," said Flair. "And when we went to check the mirrors in 'What You Are' in Sanctification, I was clean! So clean you wouldn't believe it!"

"Oh, yes we would," said Josie. "That's what happened to us, you see."

"It's amazing, just amazing!" said Flair.

"I know," agreed Josie. "I remember when I first looked at myself when I was no longer cracked and broken. The Lord Jesus made me completely, perfectly whole!¹"

"Awesome!" said Dusty again.

"I think I know now why Mr Mustardpot wanted us all to learn the Truth of Sanctification," continued Flair eagerly. "If you're not a

Christian and you visit Sanctification, then you will learn how God really sees you in the 'What You Are' mirrors – the way I did. And if you *are* a Christian, if you are set apart in practice, like the 'What You Do' of Sanctification says you should be, then God can use you to do great things – because you're focussed just on Him and listening to Him! The way the Mustardseeds have been, you see?"

The Mustardseeds stared at Flair in some amazement. They had been so focussed on their plans, and doing the right thing to help in the defence of Aletheia, that they had been practising Sanctification without even knowing it. They had so filled their time praying and thinking about the defeat of the enemies of Aletheia, that they had not paid much heed to Team WondERRful and the Revolting Nations Agreement which had taken hold of so many of their friends.

"I never even thought about how we've been set apart by being the Mustardseeds!" said Timmy.

"Remember what we thought when we visited Sanctification?" said Hugo. "If we practise being set apart to do what God wants us to do, we won't be bothered about anything else!"

Flair looked very pleased with the Mustardseeds' – and Timmy's – approval.

"This is great!" enthused Dusty. "Just great! You're well and truly one of us now, Flair!"

"I really am a proper member of the Mustardseeds, aren't I?" said Flair.

"Uh, do we need to vote on that or something?" asked Hugo.

"Of course not!" said Henrietta crisply. "Flair's in!"

"Noted," said Josie, scribbling on her notepad.

"Thanks!" smiled Flair.

The meeting continued with the Mustardseeds update reports. Hugo and Timmy, and Flair of course, had a less than promising update from their research visits to The Outskirts. They had been to many of the housing developments on The Outskirts of Aletheia, trying to conduct their survey about prayer. They had amused the people in Take-It-Easy Luxury Housing, who weren't aware of any unmet prayer need. They had annoyed the folk in Doubt Development, who were quite certain you couldn't be completely sure about anything. They got an earful of bitter abuse from the folk at the far-flung Blame-Someone-Else Housing (coming away with the distinct impression that they, the Mustardseeds, were to blame for all the problems in Aletheia). And they hadn't been able to get into No-Witness Apartments at all. Zek wished Jack was there to hear the bit about No-Witness Apartments. He and Jack knew things that Hugo didn't know about that place. They knew about the secret door. But since the two boys had decided not to tell the other Mustardseeds about their failed attempt to capture a Meddler, and about overhearing the Meddlers' silly song, Zek remained silent.

There was something puzzling about Christians who had blocked the view of the cross from their lives, and lived at a distance from everything they had trusted in for their eternal salvation. But it seemed that their distance from the cross was the reason the folk on The Outskirts could not be reached and urged to pray. Not even about the awful threat of Meddlers and Fretters. In fact, it seemed they hardly believed there was a problem in Aletheia at all, and they dismissed the evidence of dead Fretters strewn across the farmlands as some kind of spring blight on the crops. Hugo and Timmy were inclined to give up their research at The Outskirts as a hopeless cause. It seemed, in any case, hardly necessary to continue now that the Fretters had been destroyed.

"I wonder why The Outskirts people don't care enough about the Truth of Aletheia," said Henrietta.

"It's because they don't live near the cross," said Flair, who was now very keen on the subject. "And because they don't live close enough to the cross, they don't remember what the Lord Jesus did there!"

"It's because the folk in The Outskirts aren't practising the Truth of Sanctification, isn't it?" said Josie thoughtfully.

"That's it, Jo!" said Hugo. "I couldn't put my finger on what's wrong with them. But I think that must be it! They're not living lives set apart from other things, and close to the cross, and focussed on what God wants them to do. So they've become pretty useless Christians!"

"I think there's a reason Sanctification is located so near to the cross," observed Timmy.

The meeting continued, and Dusty reported that the Prayer Power Monitor was slowly growing in strength every day. The destruction of Fretters on the farmlands had had an unforeseen effect on other groups of Fretters in Aletheia. Whilst other Fretters had not been completely destroyed, they seemed to be defeated and their numbers had decreased. The old prayer-warriors from the Run-the-Race Retirement Home, released from the assault of Fretters, once more began to pray.

Dusty also mentioned some strange recordings on the Water Sensor machine, but none of the Mustardseeds knew what this meant. They didn't have the faintest idea about this device.

Henrietta and Josie had good news from the Prayer Academy. The Care-Caster Room was already half empty, and they had stood and watched several people claim the promises of God and cast their burdens into the middle of the limitless pit and leave them alone. People were released from, and were defeating, Fretters who caused them to fish with their cares instead of casting them away. More people were beginning to think less of themselves, and pray for other people instead. The Lost Property Room had fewer aimless prayers; the open portals of Sanctification had a steady stream of people visiting the 'What You Do' room and practising being clean and set apart for God to use. On the whole, the tide had turned in Aletheia's favour.

Zek, perched on the bale he once shared with Jack, enjoyed the meeting, particularly watching Hector and Flair taking it in turns to drink from her lemonade glass without either noticing the other. Hugo tried to maintain control of the more jovial attitude of the meeting, but everyone was too happy at the victories in Aletheia to pay their leader much heed. The farmland Fretters were utterly destroyed; and no one had heard a cheep from a Meddler since that memorable night. Flair talked too much throughout the meeting. Henrietta was on the verge of hysterical giggles every time Flair looked adoringly at Timmy. Timmy didn't notice the girls at all. Dusty gave a positive reaction to just about every contribution, whether sensible or otherwise. And Josie wrote notes. The Mustardseeds were still in business. The plan of the Meddlers was not yet done.

CHAPTER 27
JACK'S LEGACY

It was calm and pleasant in Aletheia following the destruction of the Fretters. Bit by bit the farmers washed their crops and trees and animals clean of the dead Fretter goo, and were cautiously optimistic about the harvest that summer.

"But it's not what it needs to be," Mr Straw confided to Zek. "We'll still be weaker than we would have been without the Fretter attack. The Fretter goo has taken some of the goodness away, you see."

Zek understood enough to realise that, while Aletheia had survived the Meddlers' plan to ruin the food supplies, the city was still weakened by the plan.

"It'll all come good if we don't suffer another attack until we're stronger," said Mr Straw. "If only the Meddlers just let us be!"

Zek thought about the wicked imps that delighted in chaos and misery. He doubted the Meddlers would leave the city of Aletheia to regain her strength before their next attack.

"If only we knew where the next attack might come," sighed Mr Straw.

It was as if a light suddenly turned on in Zek's head. "We tried to find the Meddler Pod," he said slowly, "Jack and me – we went on a mission." He explained their curious adventure, which took them to the overgrown jungle around No-Witness Apartments. He told Mr Straw about the odd man, Dim View, who had led them to the Meddlers' choir practice in the middle of a prickly gorse bush. He explained their escape from there.

"I think you found it!" said Mr Straw. "I think you found the Meddler Pod! The Rescuers searched everywhere they could, but there weren't many Rescuers left in Aletheia. I don't think it would have occurred to them the Meddlers could have settled there!"

"I think if I was a Meddler," said Zek thoughtfully, "that's where I'd choose to be. The people there are so...so scared of everything, you see?"

"Yes," agreed Mr Straw. "But the song they sang," he continued eagerly. "Do you remember the song?"

Zek shook his head sadly. "I think God did answer our prayers for that mission after all," he said. "But I never thought about it until now. We prayed that we would capture a Meddler so that we could interrogate them and learn their plans. But instead, maybe God gave us the Meddlers' song – but now I've forgotten the words!"

Mr Straw tried not to let his keen disappointment show to his young friend. "Just try and remember anything at all," he urged gently. He knew what Zek didn't know. He knew that the managers of Aletheia had renewed their efforts to locate that Meddler Pod and learn about the Meddlers' future plans. He doubted the Meddlers would still be close to No-Witness Apartments. And he was convinced that the song of the Meddlers, which Zek had described as "silly", was the key to their future plans.

Zek drank milk at Mr Straw's kitchen table and tried very hard to think. But he wasn't as good at details as Jack. And Jack was nowhere near to help him. He opened their scruffy folder and flicked idly through the pages and notes that his friend, Jack, had painstakingly copied and patiently gathered. "It's no good," he said. "Jack's gone, and I can't remember any of the words..."

But suddenly he stopped.

Slowly he pulled a torn, crumpled sheet of paper from the stack. It was Jack's slanting, precarious handwriting that was scrawled across it. Mr Straw picked up the piece of paper as if it was the most precious record in the whole of Aletheia.

Perhaps it was.

Jack Merryweather had recorded the song of the Meddlers.

CHAPTER 28
THE SONG OF THE MEDDLERS

Once more the managers of Aletheia met behind closed doors deep in the fortress of the Academy of Soldiers-of-the-Cross. They no longer met as strangers; many were now close friends. They had prayed and toiled and worked together for the defence of the city of Truth. And none knew better than Chief Steadfast, the man in charge of the whole of Aletheia, that there was so much more to do. They had gained small victories against their enemies, but they were weak and unprepared for a longer war. Any small advantage was important, and when Croft Straw carefully passed the tatty, stained piece of paper to the Chief, he handled it as if it were more precious than gold.

There was silence in the room while the Chief examined the paper. They all knew what it purported to be. It was the song of the Meddlers; perhaps it revealed the next phase of their nefarious plan for the downfall of Aletheia.

Captain Ready Steadfast, the Chief's son, leaned over the paper with the Chief. Candour Communique watched surreptitiously as Mr Straw fiddled nervously with a coffee cup, and snapped off yet another delicate china handle. She wondered how many china cups Croft had broken over the course of these frequent Management Meetings.

Philologus Mustardpot and Dr Theo Pentone flanked their colleague, Croft Straw, clearly as anxious as he. Candour could not help but notice that Dr Pentone was once more wearing his bizarre slippers. Philologus, perhaps in an attempt to cheer up his nervous friend, murmured, "Despite the fact they didn't make an entry, I'm going to award the one hundred house points for the Importance of Sanctification and Prayer assignment to the Mustardseeds, Croft. The best example of practical Sanctification and prayer that I've seen in a long time!"

Croft Straw smiled. It was nice to have some good news about his young friends. "I don't know where we'd be without them," he said.

"I think," said the Chief at last, "that we have much to thank God for. We have here, I believe, a hint at where we can expect the next phase of the attack on Aletheia."

There was a collective sigh of cautious relief at his words, and yet the Chief looked so grave that they dreaded to know what the paper had revealed.

"Sagacia," said the Chief, carefully passing the precious piece of paper to the Chief Judge, "I'd like your opinion on its meaning, please."

Chief Judge Steady took the paper and peered through her glasses at the words. She took her time, thinking, pondering, and then she slowly nodded her head. "I think we can discount the small note at the end about 'training Hector to catch Fretters'," she said rather fondly.

Mr Hardy Wallop smiled.

"Uh, yes, by all means," said the Chief. "Read out the relevant section to us, please, Sagacia."

She read the song of the Meddlers, as recorded by Jack Merryweather:

> "They squabble and they do not pray
>
> The poison-blight will come [will come!]
>
> The Meddlers' plan is here to stay
>
> Aletheia will succumb [succumb! succumb! succumb!]
>
> And now our cunning they will know
>
> The city walls will fall [will fall!]
>
> Aletheia is brought low, so low!
>
> No drinkie-drink at all! [at all! no drinkie-drink at all!]"

There was a moment of silence when the Chief Judge finished reading the song. It was, of course, a very silly song. And when it was sung by the Meddlers, who certainly could not sing, it was even sillier. But no one laughed. No one thought it was funny at all.

"Does that mean what I think it means?" asked Mr Sturdy Wright, Head Keeper of the Water of Sound Doctrine. He sounded horrified.

"I'm afraid so, Sturdy," said the Chief. "My understanding is that the first part of the song, about poison-blight, was about the Fretters attacking the crops. Thankfully, this is past. The next part, referring to 'city walls' is an attack on…"

"On our boundaries! On the Water of Sound Doctrine!" said Candour Communique, suddenly comprehending what that might mean.

Slowly the Chief nodded his head.

"That's my take on it too, Chief," said Sagacia Steady. "They will seek to attack the Water of Sound Doctrine at our boundaries. And then they will attack the sources of the Water of Sound Doctrine, perhaps even at the cross."

Sturdy Wright had gone very pale. As Head Keeper of the Water of Sound Doctrine he was in charge of the considerable team of people who safeguarded the water and kept it pure and clean for the Christians of Aletheia. If the water was polluted – then the Bible Truth they held so dear was in dreadful peril. It would no longer be the balanced Water of Sound Doctrine that was found in the Bible: it would become something else instead!

"Once more, through the goodness of God, we are forewarned of what is coming," said the Chief. "We have much to plan and prepare for!"

Aletheia was weakened but not yet overwhelmed. The real attack was coming.

For the song of the Meddlers had already begun.

EPILOGUE

Jack awoke in hospital. His head felt distinctly fuzzy. He must have been sleeping for a long, long time. And what strange dreams he had had! Was it all a dream? But where was Zek? He certainly wasn't the boy in the next hospital bed. Why had the ward changed? And that nurse he could see without moving his head was definitely *not* one of those who reported to the colourful Dr Pentone.

"Where am I?" he muttered.

Mum immediately placed her cool hand on his forehead. "In the hospital, Jack," she said soothingly. "You picked up a strange infection and they brought you here. Do you remember anything?"

"F-Fretters," mumbled Jack.

Mum shook her head helplessly. "So you kept saying in your sleep," she said. "The school don't seem to know anything about it! They said they found you ill in the classroom after morning break, when you'd been on classroom cleaning duty! And the doctors here are quite baffled..."

"Fretters," mumbled Jack again.

"Yes," said Mum calmly. "Well, never mind that just now, I'll go and let the nurse know you're awake. I must say you really do look on the mend at last!"

Mum left, and Harris, Jack's little brother, approached from the foot of the hospital bed, carrying a half-empty box of chocolates. "They sent you presents from school," he explained, offering Jack one of the chocolates. Jack shook his head. He still felt like he imagined a blight-poisoned blossom tree might feel; and that definitely didn't include wanting chocolate.

"They sent you a card too," said Harris. "It says, 'Made by Marigold Goody' on the back."

Jack didn't care much about the card either. "I don't think it was all just a dream," he said, still seeing visions of angry, biting, poisonous Fretters.

"Was it another trip to Aletheia, Jack?" asked Harris hesitantly. "Is that what happened?" Harris had great faith in Jack's stories about Aletheia.

"It was Aletheia," said Jack, sitting up, his clouded mind beginning to remember.

Harris' eyes were round with curiosity and wonder. "What happened, Jack?"

"Aletheia is under attack," said Jack distinctly. He lifted his bandaged hands.

"Mum said some bug must have bitten you," said Harris, eyeing the bandages. "That's how you got sick."

"I need to go back to Aletheia and help them," said Jack.

"Can I come too?" asked Harris.

"It's dangerous," said Jack.

"How will you get back?"

"Timmy said it was called *Underground Entry*," said Jack. "Somehow I'm going to find it."

"I'll help you look," said Harris.

"The Meddlers' song!" Jack suddenly exclaimed.

"Was it a nice song?" asked Harris.

Jack shook his head. "But it's important," he said, "I know that now. I wrote it down. I hope the Mustardseeds find it."

"The Mustardseeds," repeated Harris with interest. "Could I be one of them?"

Jack was about to say 'no' (which was the standard answer for Harris), when he stopped and considered. The mustard seed was tiny. It was nothing at all. It was God who was great. It was God who made the difference. It didn't matter how small or insignificant you were; if you placed all of your confidence in God, you could do great things, even conquer the foes of Aletheia!

He contemplated his answer. "I think," he said at last, "I think anyone can be a mustard seed."

REFERENCES

Unless otherwise stated, all Bible references are taken from the New King James Version of the Bible.

1. [References on pages 22, 50 (2), 56, 64, 88, 89, 138, 146, 152, 180, 229] You can read about this in Book 3 of the Aletheia Adventure Series, The Broken Journey.

2. [Reference on page 23] The Bible teaches that all of the words in the Bible come from God, and therefore they are the Word of God. A verse that describes this is **2 Timothy 3:16-17**:
   "All Scripture is given by inspiration of God, and is profitable for doctrine, for reproof, for correction, for instruction in righteousness, that the man of God may be complete, thoroughly equipped for every good work."

3. [Reference on page 26] This is a reference to the story in the Bible when God opened the mouth of a donkey and the donkey spoke. You can read about this in **Numbers 22:22-35**.

4. [References on pages 30, 43] 'Sin' is the Bible name for all the

wrong things that everyone has done. The Bible teaches everyone has sinned against God.

There is a verse about this in **Romans 3:23**:

"For all have sinned and fall short of the glory of God."

5. [Reference on page 43] There are many verses in the Bible which explain how to become a Christian. Here are a couple of examples:

    Acts 16:31:

    "Believe on the Lord Jesus Christ, and you will be saved."

    Romans 10:9:

    "If you confess with your mouth the Lord Jesus and believe in your heart that God has raised Him from the dead, you will be saved."

6. [References on pages 43, 181, 190] The Bible shows that the Lord Jesus came to pay the price for the sin of the whole world. He paid to God the debt that everyone owes for all their sins. However, only people who trust in Him will have their sins taken away. Here are examples of verses about this:

    1 John 2:2:

    "And He Himself [the Lord Jesus] is the propitiation for our sins, and not for ours only but also for the whole world."

['propitiation' means the turning away of God's anger at sin because He was so pleased with the sacrifice of the Lord Jesus]

John 1:29:

"John saw Jesus coming toward him, and said, 'Behold! The Lamb of God who takes away the sin of the world!'"

John 3:16:

"For God so loved the world that He gave His only begotten Son, that whoever believes in Him should not perish but have everlasting life."

7. [References on pages 44, 54, 127] Having faith as a mustard seed is a reference to a verse in the Bible:

Matthew 17:20:

"So Jesus said to them..."I say to you, if you have faith as a mustard seed, you will say to this mountain, 'Move from here to there,' and it will move; and nothing will be impossible for you."

8. [References on pages 44, 168] There are verses in the Bible which explain that God will answer prayer when we ask something in keeping with His will (God's will is always in keeping with the

Bible). Here are some examples:

John 14:13-14:

"And whatever you ask in My name, that I will do, that the Father may be glorified in the Son. If you ask anything in My name, I will do it."

John 15:16:

"I chose you and appointed you that you should go and bear fruit, and that your fruit should remain, that whatever you ask the Father in My name He may give you."

1 John 3:22:

"And whatever we ask we receive from Him [God], because we keep His commandments and do those things that are pleasing in His sight."

1 John 5:14:

"Now this is the confidence that we have in Him [God], that if we ask anything according to His will, He hears us."

9. [References on pages 49, 197] You can read about this in Book 1 of the Aletheia Adventure Series, The Rescue of Timmy Trial.

10. [Reference on page 83] This is a quote from **Psalm 40:11**:

"Do not withhold Your tender mercies from me, O Lord;

Let Your lovingkindness and Your truth continually preserve me."

11. [References on pages 106, 183] The Bible teaches that, as much as possible, Christians should be like the Lord Jesus. The more I am like the Lord Jesus, the better God is pleased. And one day those who are Christians will be made like Him completely. Here are a few references to this subject in the Bible:

Ephesians 5:1-2:

"Therefore be imitators of God as dear children. And walk in love, as Christ also has loved us and given Himself for us, an offering and a sacrifice to God for a sweet-smelling aroma."

Philippians 2:5:

"Let this mind be in you which was also in Christ Jesus."

Romans 8:28-29:

"And we know that all things work together for good to those who love God, to those who are the called according to His purpose. For whom He foreknew, He also predestined to be conformed to the image of His Son."

1 John 3:2:

"Beloved, now we are children of God; and it has not yet been revealed what we shall be, but we know that when He is revealed, we shall be like Him, for we shall see Him as He is."

12. [Reference on page 127] The Bible teaches that with God nothing is impossible. Here are a couple of verses from the Bible about this.
Luke 1:37:

"For with God nothing will be impossible."

Luke 18:27:

"But He [the Lord Jesus] said, "The things which are impossible with men are possible with God.""

13. [References on pages 139, 198] The Bible talks about Christians putting on the 'armour of God'.
This is explained in **Ephesians 6:10-18**:

"Finally, my brethren, be strong in the Lord and in the power of His might.

Put on the whole armour of God, that you may be able to stand against the wiles of the devil. For we do not wrestle against flesh and blood, but against principalities, against powers, against the rulers of the darkness of this age, against spiritual hosts of wickedness in the heavenly places. Therefore take up the whole armour of God, that you may be able to withstand in the evil day, and having done all, to stand.

Stand therefore, having girded your waist with truth, having put on the breastplate of righteousness, and having shod your feet with the preparation of the gospel of peace; above all, taking the shield of faith with which you will be able to quench all the fiery darts of the wicked one. And take the helmet of salvation, and the sword of the Spirit, which is the word of God; praying always with all prayer and supplication in the Spirit..."

14. [Reference on page 156] This is a reference to **Galatians 6:2**: "Bear one another's burdens, and so fulfil the law of Christ."

15. [References on pages 156, 159] This is a reference to **1 Peter 5:7**: "Casting all your care upon Him [God], for He [God] cares for you."

16. [Reference on page 167 (2)] You can read about this in Book 2 of the Aletheia Adventure Series, The Purple Storm.

17. [Reference on page 167] **James 5:16-18** is a verse about God answering prayer:

"The effective, fervent prayer of a righteous man avails much.

Elijah was a man with a nature like ours, and he prayed earnestly that it would not rain; and it did not rain on the land for three years and six months.

And he prayed again, and the heaven gave rain, and the earth produced its fruit."

18. [Reference on page 179] When we trust in the Lord Jesus, He washes us clean from everything we have done wrong. We are then completely clean and right in God's sight.

This is explained in **1 John 1:7**:

"And the blood of Jesus Christ His [God's] Son cleanses us from all sin."

19. [Reference on page 179] When we trust in the Lord Jesus and are cleansed from our sins the Lord Jesus becomes our righteousness. ['Righteous' just means to be completely right]. So, when we are saved, the Lord Jesus, Who is completely right and perfect, covers us in His own rightness, and then God sees us completely right and perfect because of the Lord Jesus. Here are some verses about this.

2 Corinthians 5:21:

"For He made Him who knew no sin to be sin for us, that we might become the righteousness of God in Him."

Philippians 3:9:

"And be found in Him, not having my own righteousness, which is from the law, but that which is through faith in Christ, the righteousness which is from God by faith."

20. [Reference on page 182] The Bible teaches that, even if we are Christians, we need to be cleansed daily and continually from the effects of sin on us. The Lord Jesus taught this when He washed His disciples' feet. You can read about this in **John 13:1-17**. There are also other verses about the need for Christians to be continually cleaned by the Bible and prayer, such as:

2 Corinthians 7:1:

"Let us cleanse ourselves from all filthiness of the flesh and spirit, perfecting holiness in the fear of God."

1 John 1:9:

If we confess our sins, He is faithful and just to forgive us our sins and to cleanse us from all unrighteousness."

21. [Reference on page 182] The Bible teaches that when God saves a person and they become a Christian, He gives them a new life. God has 'sanctified' (or separated) people who trust in Him to live a different kind of life, in a different kind of way. They are 'set apart' for Him. Some verses which help to explain this are:

2 Corinthians 5:17:

"Therefore, if anyone is in Christ, he is a new creation; old things have passed away; behold, all things have become new."

2 Corinthians 6:14, 16, 17:

"Do not be unequally yoked together with unbelievers...

For you are the temple of the living God...

Therefore

"Come out from among them

And be ye separate, says the Lord.

Do not touch what is unclean,

And I will receive you.""

1 Thessalonians 5:23:

"Now may the God of peace Himself sanctify you completely; and may your whole spirit, soul, and body be preserved blameless at the coming of our Lord Jesus Christ."

22. [Reference on page 184] This is a reference to a verse in the Bible which explains that in the future, when Christians go to heaven to be with the Lord Jesus, they shall be like Him. If we remember this, it will keep us right and encourage us as Christians on earth.

You can read about this in **1 John 3:2-3**:

"Beloved, now we are children of God; and it has not yet been revealed what we shall be, but we know that when He is revealed, we shall be like Him, for we shall see Him as He is. And everyone who has this hope in Him purifies himself ['himself' means men and women here], just as He is pure."

23. [Reference on page 190] The Bible teaches that there is only one way to be right with God, and that is through the Lord Jesus. The Lord Jesus is the mediator – that is, He has made provision for anyone who trusts in Him to come back to God. This is explained in:

1 Timothy 2:5:

"For there is one God and one Mediator between God and men, the Man Christ Jesus."

[Note that 'men' here means all people]

The Lord Jesus also said that He was the way back to God.

This can be found in **John 14:6**:

"Jesus said to him, "I am the way, the truth, and the life. No one comes to the Father except through Me.""

24. [Reference on page 196] This is a reference to a verse in **Psalm 119:105** which explains how the Bible can show us the way as a light:

"Your word is a lamp to my feet

And a light to my path."

[The Bible doesn't mean that the Bible is a literal light; this verse is saying that the Word of God will be our guide through life if we believe what the Bible says.]

25. [Reference on page 224] The Bible tells us many things about the character of God and how great He is. Here are a few examples of how great God is and why we can trust in Him:

a) God is our Creator and designed us to be in communion with Him and to trust in Him (Genesis chapters 1 and 2);

b) God is above all and rules over everything (Psalm 83:18; Psalm 92:8; Daniel 4:17);

c) God sees everything (Hebrews 4:13);

d) God knows everything (Psalm 147:5);

e) God cannot lie, and always keeps His promises (Titus 1:2; Hebrews 10:23; 2 Peter 3:9);

f) God does not change (Malachi 3:6);

g) God is love and always seeks the best for us (1 John 4:8; Jeremiah 31:3; John 3:16);

h) God is faithful and has promised to forgive us on the basis of what the Lord Jesus has done (1 John 1:9).